Teens Go Green!

Recent Titles in
Libraries Unlimited Professional Guides for Young Adult Librarians
C. Allen Nichols and Mary Anne Nichols, Series Editors

Serving Young Teens and 'Tweens
Sheila B. Anderson, editor

The Guy-Friendly Teen Library: Serving Male Teens
Rollie Welch

Serving Urban Teens
Paula Brehm-Heeger

The Teen-Centered Writing Club: Bringing Teens and Words Together
Constance Hardesty

More Than MySpace: Teens, Librarians, and Social Networking
Robyn Lupa, Editor

Visual Media for Teens: Creating and Using a Teen-Centered Film Collection
Jane Halsall and R. William Edminster

Teen-Centered Library Service: Putting Youth Participation into Practice
Diane P. Tuccillo

Booktalking with Teens
Kristine Mahood

Make Room for Teens!: Reflections on Developing Teen Spaces in Libraries
Michael G. Farrelly

Teens, Libraries, and Social Networking: What Librarians Need to Know
Denise E. Agosto and June Abbas, Editors

Starting from Scratch: Building a Teen Library Program
Sarah Ludwig

Serving Teen Parents: From Literacy Skills to Life Skills
Ellin Klor and Sarah Lapin

Teens Go Green!

Tips, Techniques, Tools, and Themes for YA Programming

Valerie Colston

Libraries Unlimited Professional Guides for Young Adult Librarians
C. Allen Nichols and Mary Anne Nichols, Series Editors

AN IMPRINT OF ABC-CLIO, LLC
Santa Barbara, California • Denver, Colorado • Oxford, England

Copyright 2012 by Valerie Colston

Library of Congress Cataloging-in-Publication Data

Colston, Valerie.
  Teens go green! : tips, techniques, tools, and themes for YA programming /
Valerie Colston.
      p. cm. — (Libraries Unlimited professional guides for young adult librarians)
  Includes bibliographical references and index.
  ISBN 978-1-59158-929-7 (acid-free paper) — ISBN 978-1-59158-930-3 (ebook)
1. Young adults' libraries—Activity programs—United States.   2. Environmental
education—Activity programs—United States.   3. Libraries and teenagers—
United States.   I. Title.
  Z718.5.C627   2012
  027.62'6—dc23   2011029006

ISBN: 978-1-59158-929-7
EISBN: 978-1-59158-930-3

16 15 14 13 12   1 2 3 4 5

This book is also available on the World Wide Web as an eBook.
Visit www.abc-clio.com for details.

Libraries Unlimited
An Imprint of ABC-CLIO, LLC

ABC-CLIO, LLC
130 Cremona Drive, P.O. Box 1911
Santa Barbara, California 93116-1911

This book is printed on acid-free paper ∞

Manufactured in the United States of America

CONTENTS

Series Foreword vii
Acknowledgments ix
Introduction xi

PART I: GOING GREEN

**Chapter 1—What You Need to Go Green: Basic Supplies
and General Resources** 3
What Green Looks Like 3
A Supply of Supplies 4
Basic Materials 4

Chapter 2—Teaching Tips, Themes, and Formats 11
Tips for Teaching Teens 11
Green Themes: Where Do You Find Them? 13

Chapter 3—Making It Techno-Green: Techie Spaces, Blogs, and Websites 15
The Theme 15
Imagination 15
Resources for Green Spaces 16

**Chapter 4—Sharing the Green: Marketing Programs at Your Home Library
and on the Road** 19
Create a Club 19
How to Start a Library Club 20

PART II: ART PROGRAMS AND PROJECTS

Chapter 5—Simply Inexpensive One Hour Eco-Friendly Art Programs 27
Fabulous Paper Fashion 28
Sassy Grassy Grass Portraits 31
Dancers Paper Style 34

Recycled Cars 37
Music Box (from a Recycled Book) 41
Camouflage Catch All 44

Chapter 6—Fast-Food Containers and Other Toss-Aways **49**
After Juice Aftershave 50
Drink It and Grow It: Plant It in the Library 53
Eat It! Paint It! 56
Gumball or Candy Machine Replica 59

Chapter 7—Green Themes for a Greenback: Art Projects for Under $1.00 . . . . **63**
Desktop Organizer with Fake Spill 64
Way Cool Bark Jewelry 67
Let's Get Physical: Weights 70
Your State Bird 74

Chapter 8—Green Teen Get-Togethers: All-Nighters, Afterschool, and More **77**
T-Shirt All-Nighter 78
Fashion Redux 81
Night at the Museum 84
Eco Group Shadow Sculpture 85
Eight-Pack Soda Ring Quilt Throw 88

**Chapter 9—Going Local and Global: International, Community,
and Intergenerational Art Projects** **91**
Cats and Dogs: Art for a Cause 92
Picasso-Inspired International Green Cards 95
Christmas around the World 99
Zulu Love Bead Doll 103

Chapter 10—Earth Day and Other Celebration Ideas All Year Long **107**
Go Global Eco Globes 108
Architecture in a Box: Design a New Architectural Style and Future
City Using Packaging Material 111
Globe-Trotting Habitat Float 114
Under-the-Sea Creatures 117
Water Fountain—Table Style 120
Save a Squirrel 123

Chapter 11—Books into Art Programs **127**
Neighborhood Bird Study Program—Audubon Style 128
Trash to Treasure Arts Party 132
Photographing the Wetlands (or Other Natural Wonders) 135
Green Jobs: What and Where Are They? 138

Index 139

SERIES FOREWORD

Many of us are becoming more aware of ways we can save the earth's resources and how to incorporate those actions in our daily lives. Libraries are no different and many are "going green" in building construction and services. We are very excited that Valerie Colston has written *Teens Go Green! Tips, Techniques, Tools, and Themes for YA Programming* as the newest addition to our series. Colston has provided a treasure trove of wonderful art projects to use with teens. This unique guide provides practical and creative easy-to-follow projects for the librarian. Teens will love the eco-friendly art and have fun in programs while helping the environment.

We are proud of our association with Libraries Unlimited/ABC-CLIO, which continues to prove itself as the premier publisher of books to help library staff serve teens. This series has succeeded because our authors know the needs of those library employees who work with young adults. Without exception, they have written useful and practical handbooks for library staff.

We hope you find this book, as well as our entire series, to be informative, providing you with valuable ideas as you serve teens and that this work will further inspire you to do great things to make teens welcome in your library. If you have an idea for a title that could be added to our series, or would like to submit a book proposal, please email us at lu-books@lu.com. We'd love to hear from you.

Mary Anne Nichols
C. Allen Nichols

ACKNOWLEDGMENTS

For the inspiration of this book and her suggestions I would like to thank RoseMary Honnold, a name synonymous with teen library programming.

Thank you to Barbara Ittner, senior acquisitions editor, for her enthusiasm on the subject, and to my editor, C. Allen Nichols, for his support, ideas, attention to detail, and encouragement.

There are librarians who see the value of inviting artists and performers into their space, making the library an even more magical place for children and teens. One of the first librarians to invite me into her world many years ago with my art was Zelda Sacro-Santo, children's librarian at the Rancho Bernardo Library, a community of San Diego, California. There are other Youth Service Librarians (YSL) who deserve a shout-out for their insight and enthusiasm; they are Eileen Labrador, Judy Cunningham, Sandra Coleman, Lisa Burget, Joyce McMaster, Erwin Magbanua, and the others who deserve recognition for all they do.

We wouldn't know about the many artists, musicians, storytellers, and others who have talents to share without the organizers who work hard to give performers an opportunity to audition and advertise. Sharon Henegar, coordinator of children's services of the Orange County Public Library, and Jennifer Lawson, teen specialist for San Diego County Library, are especially effective and hardworking in this area.

Thank you to the many children's and teen librarians who have taken the time to attend my *Art for the Youth Librarians* workshops online. It's always amazing to see so many willing to learn art skills (on their own time) and share those ideas with their young adult patrons. I appreciate the networking and sharing of ideas.

Thank you to Kandice for showing me how truly entertaining packing material can be for creating spectacular architecture—I "heart" you—and the very creative Drisana, Andrew, Tasha, Izzy, Sebby, Crystal, Cameron, Kylie, Cara, Chris, Preston, Matthew, and Cathlene.

For all the things he is, much appreciation to my son, Joe; and to him, his wife, Maricel, and the very sweet newest edition, Troy Maximo Colston, much love.

This book is dedicated to Joy Lee Cole, our mom who left this world much too early but gave us the gift of each other. So, thank you, mom, for my brothers and sisters and life-long friends, Ken Bradshaw, Mike Cole, David Cole, Cindy Cole, and Coleen Cole, and their spouses, Minda, Pat, Steve, and Jon.

INTRODUCTION

Make the library relevant to young people! Increase teen participation! Work within your budget limitations! Young adult librarians, already challenged with a long list of demands, now have a new charge, *make it green.*

As an art professor and in my role as a library art performer for more than two decades, I have seen firsthand the ability of YA librarians to adapt and expand their roles offering innovative and meaningful service to their teen patrons. My *Art for Youth Librarians* online workshops have been filled with those who are eager to learn art skills and new ideas to create a variety of programming for this age group. Youth service personnel are already equipped with enthusiasm and creativity, but they would like the confidence that comes through training. YA librarians seek projects and programming that are fulfilling, meaningful, and fun to the populations they serve.

It's the savvy librarian who can take on the challenge of presenting meaningful and substantive green programming. This practical book presents easy-to-follow, step-by-step instructions that are essential to bringing successful eco-friendly art programs to your library.

WHY SHOULD YOU CARE?

Teens of the 21st century are some of the most environmentally aware individuals you will meet. They have not been labeled *generation green* without earning it. Television and motion picture media, the Internet, and their educational curriculum have educated them about climate change, global warming, endangered species, and the need for alternative-energy programs. Teens know their ecological footprint—do you? It takes creative and ecologically astute youth librarians and teachers to provide challenging and interesting programming to their young library patrons and students. Young adult leaders want to make a difference, but the challenge is *how.* How can you create educationally sound and fun art programming?

Why should young adult librarians concern themselves with environmentally sound art programs that promote green art projects? Who benefits? What does a "green" program look like? What supplies will you need? How do you reach and teach this particular age group? These questions will be answered, and practical art projects and programming ideas will be presented in this book.

ART AND ECOLOGY

Public school and library art programs have always been vulnerable targets for budget cuts in the best of times, but the financial crisis of the first decade of the 21st century has forced the closure of many libraries and has at the same time eliminated art programs in many schools. At the same time awareness of the importance of addressing ecological concerns has never been more on the minds of people old and young. For the socially aware young adult group, going green is not just a commercial slogan or a political discussion but a real call to action. Young adults are looking for enthusiastic and informed adults to lead the way.

Here are just a few interesting ecological quotes:

500 billion to 1 trillion plastic bags are consumed worldwide each year. The city of San Francisco will be first city in the U.S. to take a stand and ban plastic bags in large markets and pharmacies.

—Craftzine Blog,
http://blog.craftzine.com/archive/2007/08/
plastic_bag_crafts.html

If you had a 15-year-old tree and made it into paper grocery bags, you'd get about 700 of them. A busy supermarket could use all of them in under an hour! This means in one year, one supermarket can go through over 6 million paper bags! Imagine how many supermarkets there are just in the United States!!!

The average household throws away 13,000 separate pieces of paper each year. Most is packaging and junk mail.

Americans use 2,500,000 plastic bottles every hour! Most of them are thrown away!

—Recycling Revolution Website,
http://www.recycling-revolution.com/
recycling-facts.html

LIBRARIES WITH BENEFITS

They will come, so you need to build it. More communities are depending on the library for a variety of teen activities. The neighborhood library has been asked to provide a safe haven for afterschool teens who may have few choices when it comes to positive activities. At the same time, a greater demand has been placed on youth librarians. They have been asked to develop and teach arts and crafts programming. Expectations from library administration, the community, and teens are high. With the reduction of funds for on-site school programs, teachers and school administrators are depending on local libraries to provide electives that were once reserved district visual art curriculums.

Teens Go Green! Tips, Techniques, Tools, and Themes for YA Programming provides an easy-to-understand, practical, and hands-on guide for teachers and librarians wanting to create quality and environmentally friendly teen programming. It's like having your own art expert!

Organized into two parts, this book combines art and programming ideas with the theme of green. The first chapter outlines what you will need. Basic supplies and general resources important for creating art programs that focus on green projects will be introduced. Incorporated in chapter 2 are easy-to-understand tips and advice for teaching and designing eco-friendly art themes and formats that your tween and teen audience will enthusiastically attend. Chapter 3 introduces the important role technology plays in a successfully green-sensitive library program. Finally, rounding out Part I is chapter 4, which presents practical and unique ways to share ideas and expand teen involvement in library clubs. Innovative methods for showcasing teen art through exhibits and displays in your library and in the community are outlined.

Part II (chapters 5–11) provides practical, easy-to-follow art project ideas and illustrations that make the job of developing and teaching green teen art projects possible. Each chapter begins with an introduction outlining the general purpose, specific topics, and time frame you can expect to complete each project. Each program or project is designed especially for the teen audience and their particular interests. Lesson pages are designed to be easily accessed and read by the presenter. A photograph of the completed project is provided along with easy-to-follow instructions. The estimated cost ($$$$$ being the most expensive), suggested age level, required materials and programming ideas, professional and young adult resources, and teaching tips and suggestions, where applicable, are also included on each lesson page.

The unique aspect of this book is that it focuses on themes that are relevant, inspiring, and, most of all, fun for teens. It speaks their language with art programming ideas that include recycled car designs, group gardens, grass pets, ocean and other environmental themes, and art projects that blend social action with art appeal. This book merges the concern for "being green" with easy-to-understand art project ideas. Written by an experienced art professor, the book is organized as part advice column and part how-to resource manual.

Who's already going green? What supplies do you need? What are some of the best green resources? You will find answers to those questions and more in chapter 1.

PART I

❖ ❖ ❖

GOING GREEN

1

◄❖►◄❖►◄❖►

WHAT YOU NEED TO GO GREEN: BASIC SUPPLIES AND GENERAL RESOURCES

WHAT GREEN LOOKS LIKE

Hundreds, perhaps thousands, of libraries are going green. There are many resources and simple things that you can do to make your library and your programs green or greener.

In *The Green Library Movement: An Overview and Beyond* by Monika Antonelli outlines why libraries are choosing to go green and how their programs are reflecting environmental concerns. Books such as Kathlyn Miller's *Public Libraries Going Green* suggest it is the role of the library to educate and model good ecological behaviors and provide a number of actions to do just that.

Other libraries such as the Princeton Library have compiled healthy booklists, such as:

Teen Book List Environmental Topics Fiction & Nonfiction Books & Videos. http://www.princeton.lib.nj.us/teens/green/documents/booklist_env_teens.pdf

Need more ideas? You will find 100 more ideas to green your library at the *Green Library Blog*:

http://thegreenlibraryblog.blogspot.com/2009/05/100-ways-to-make-your-library-little.html

When you are considering greening your library programs, there are plenty of simple things to do. Here's a list of 10:

1. **Regenerate it.** Make it new again. Take an innovative approach to an old idea. Make a commitment to make green a way of life.
2. **Recycle it.** Use newspaper, plastic bottles, cartons, and containers that lend themselves to recycling projects.
3. **Reuse it.** Don't throw it out. Save it for the next program or project. Give it a double life.
4. **Resource it.** Today, there are many green voices out there with many suggestions, especially on the Internet. Blogs, websites, organizations, and books are easy to locate. Network and find information.

5. **Redo it.** Remember when you were a kid and you could declare a do-over? Take tried-and-true projects that have been successful and re-do them, this time *greener*.
6. **Replace it.** Whether it is an appliance that uses too much energy or an art pen that makes you ill, replace it with a better idea.
7. **Renew it.** Take an old idea or object and make it new again.
8. **Reclaim** your confidence. You can do it. You are more creative than you realize.
9. **Rediscover** your creative side. Start to look at things in a new way. Write down 10 things that you can create with a paper bag.
10. **Recreate** the materials around you into art with a new function.

A SUPPLY OF SUPPLIES

What will you need to go green? The basic tools you will need to produce a green art program are listed in the following sections.

Storage

An important consideration in any supply room is storage. It is a good idea to purchase and collect the following containers for storing crayons, scissors, glues, paper brads, stickers, tape, pencils, colored pencils, pens, beads, and other small items. Cans are great for mixing and blending materials also.

Cardboard shoeboxes
Recycled plastic shoeboxes
Recycled plastic containers
Recycled plastic bags
Empty coffee cans
Cardboard boxes in various sizes
Fishing tackle and tool boxes
School supply containers found at teacher supply stores
Plastic paint storage jars small and large

Storage of Brushes

Brushes should be cleaned thoroughly and dried. Use coffee cans or plastic to store cleaned brushes.

Storage of Paper Items

Large portfolio folders for prints, collage materials, and tissue craft papers
Mount posters onto card stock and laminate
Recycled boxes for additional storage components
Spiral notebooks for storing stickers, art project ideas, collage materials, and other bits and pieces
Labeled accordion and plastic files found at office supply stores

BASIC MATERIALS

Although each art project will require unique materials, there are some common materials and supplies that are basic to most creative art environments.

Papers

The Basic Necessities

Drawing paper: Plain white, heavyweight, 18 by 24 inches (20 sheets per pack or pad)
Construction paper (various colors): Black and white are especially important for drawing projects.

Newsprint paper: Lightweight, 18 by 24 inches (50 sheets per pack or pad). Newsprint is inexpensive and works well with most mediums.

Brown poster wrap, 60 lb., 30 inches by 15 yards. You can find brown shipping paper in drugstores, dollar stores, and arts and crafts stores.

Junk mail and other recyclable papers such as old magazines, stationary and office papers, gift wrap, and various packaging

Packing material: Look for materials in shipped boxes that can also be used in projects.

Tag board/poster board: white heavyweight, 10 by 13 inches

Paper plates: White thinner type

Brown bags: Small and large

Newspapers

Media

The Basic Necessities

1 quart of tempera (dry or liquid) in red, yellow, blue, white, and black

1 pint of acrylic paint in various colors (red, yellow, blue, green, purple, orange)

2 pints of acrylic paint in black and white

8 tubes of watercolors (liquid) in a variety of colors, including white

15 round natural paint brushes

15 square natural paint brushes

Can or plastic cylinder to store brushes

Crayons (1 pack per participant)

Colored chalk (1 pack per participant)

White chalk (1 piece for each participant)

Colored markers (1 pack per participant)

Felt or Pilot pens with variety of points

Black charcoal (1 piece for each participant)

Air-hardening clay (Laguna Clay Company makes a variety of air-hardening clays and provides a website with lesson plans, http://www.lagunaclay.com/classroom/projects.php. You will need two boxes of clay for a group of 15.)

Optional

Nontoxic glass paints (highly recommended)

Colored sand

Glues and Attachments

The Basic Necessities

Aleene's Glue and basic school glue (any brand)

Papier-mâché paste

School glue

Paper brads

One-hole paper punch tools

Masking tape

Variety of colored tapes

Various colored pipe cleaners

Optional

Specialty glues such as Aleene's Fabric Stiffener, Fabric Tacky Pack, and Thick Designer Tacky Glue

Binding tool and attachments

Brushes, Tools, and Art Instruments

The Basic Necessities

Assortment of brushes (easel brushes, watercolor brushes, and painting brushes)

Drawing pencils or assortment of #2 pencils

Soft erasers

Scissors (variety according to age group; left-handed and special-needs students will require additional purchasing considerations)

Craft Supplies

The Basic Necessities

Woodsie wooden shapes, 2 packages per 15 participants (You can find these popular and nostalgic crafts pieces at Woodcrafter, http://www.woodcrafter.com/woodsies.aspx)

Wooden craft sticks

Colored craft sticks

Clear straws

Felt squares, 9 by 12 inches, in a variety of colors

Beads, a variety of colors and sizes

Jute, 325 feet of twine beading string

Plastic craft string, 100 feet

Colored pasta and rice

Fabric scraps

Yarn, 221 yards (one standard skein)

Feathers

Optional

Tile mosaics

Stickers (variety)

Wood blocks and tools for shaping

Fimo clays and toaster oven

Elison shapes and cutters

Art History

Along with hands-on art projects there is a need for art history.

The Basic Necessities

Art prints (Teens can learn about art, themselves, and their world through the study of paintings and other art mediums. Inexpensive and essential art prints are an important consideration of any art room and important as a reference for teen papers.)

Selection of art history books

Art history videos

Internet access and classroom website

Safety

The Basic Necessities

Goggles (protective eyewear)

Gloves

Masks

Manufacturers' labels for safety and age warnings should be strictly followed. You can locate safety guidelines for each school district for your library. They should be posted in the art room and made available to all librarians.

 **CAUTIONARY NOTE:** Certain materials that used to be used in schools are no longer allowed. Exposure to materials such as turpentine, other solvents, adhesives such as model cement, and permanent felt tip markers can cause serious health damage, and these should not be used in a library environment.

Is Your Art Programming Safe?

Take an inventory of the art supplies you have on hand and have used in past programs. What changes do you need to make?

Recycled Materials

Your art budget will be enhanced, and teens will learn about recycling, if you incorporate the following materials into your art room supply list. It's good for the library budget and the environment.

You can ask parents and teens to help collect the following or visit local charity thrift stores for plastic bags filled with discarded treasures. Craigslist (www.craigslist.com) also offers free materials (you can often find books, boxes, and a variety of freebies for your art projects).

fabrics

ribbons

bows

buttons

beads

bottle caps

plastic water bottles

aluminum cans

old greeting cards

newspapers

magazines for collage materials

bark that has fallen from trees (this can be used to create a leather-like texture on Native American products)

rocks

feathers

acorns

leaves

fallen and dried flowers

packaging from light bulbs or other boxes

ticket stubs

postcards

seashells

carpet squares

shoeboxes

Styrofoam packaging materials

egg cartons, dry food packaging

paper shopping bags

tin cans

plastic containers

All of these items can be used for storage and mixing but also incorporated into project ideas. There are always the surprises as well, those odds and ends that are picked up at the fast-food encounter, the contents of the package after the shopping spree, and the results of the peek into the trash bin.

 **NOTE:** Teens should be reminded not to peel bark still on the tree, and should also be advised not to pick up feathers from the ground—many carry disease.

Miscellaneous

Newspapers and plastic drop cloth for covering surfaces

Smocks or old shirts to protect clothing

Aluminum tins and trays to hold paints and collage materials

Paper towels

Cloth rags and sponges

Did You Know That . . .

In recent years, a number of art and craft supplies containing toxic materials have been used in California schools. Asbestos, heavy metals, organic solvents, and other toxic ingredients found in some art and craft materials present risks to the health and safety of individuals using them.

—Office of Environmental Health Hazard Assessment
OEHHA Guidelines for the Safe Use of Arts
and Crafts Materials (updated May 2007)
http://oehha.ca.gov/education/art/artguide.html

This California government website is very helpful, listing toxic materials and making suggestions for safe substitutes. Those materials that many of us used as children are no longer considered safe to use in schools or libraries.

PROFESSIONAL RESOURCES

Antonelli, Monika. (2008). The green library movement: An overview and beyond. *Electronic Green Journal*, 1(27). Retrieved from http://escholarship.org/uc/item/39d3v236.

This article not only outlines resources written by and for librarians but also shows the concern of librarians that has turned into a green movement. Specific ideas are presented that give practical advice for those wanting to bring environmental awareness to the library community.

McKay, K., & Bonnin, J. (2007). *True green: 100 everyday ways you can contribute to a healthier planet*. Des Moines, IL: National Geographic.

Sometimes it's the little things we do that make a big difference. This book gives suggestions for changes that are easy to incorporate into your daily life and will make a big difference in the overall picture.

Miller, K. (2010). *Public libraries going green*. Chicago: American Library Association.
    Want to know what other libraries are doing to make their carbon footprint smaller? This book is for you.

Wachowiak, F., & Clements, R. (1993). *Emphasize art—A qualitative art program for elementary and middle schools*. New York: Harper Collins.
    Even though the projects are geared more toward middle school and younger, the book is a good reference tool for anyone teaching art.

Yarrow, J. (2008). *How to reduce your carbon footprint: 365 simple ways to save energy, resources, and money*. London: Duncan Baird.
    Follow these suggestions and incorporate one idea a day and you will have a carbon footprint you can brag about.

2

TEACHING TIPS, THEMES, AND FORMATS

What is a green theme, and where do you find ideas that will interest and inspire you and your young adult audience? You have some favorite programs that have always worked in the past, and now is the time to rethink their teen appeal and impact on the environment. This chapter outlines simple suggestions to consider when creating any program, past or present. But, first, how do you go about facilitating a creative environment for young adults?

TIPS FOR TEACHING TEENS

In many communities, the role of the youth librarian has expanded to include that of art educator. Not trained in the arts, youth librarians sometimes feel ill equipped to take on the role. The following tips will help.

Teen Likes and Dislikes

These are just a few observations that I have learned working with teens. I am sure you have your own.

1. Teens like to create arts and crafts that they can use and that are environmentally friendly. They want to do a good job and are proud of their creations.
2. They don't like to have too much of the spotlight placed on them alone. They need and want encouragement but would rather blend into the crowd even though they enjoy producing something unique.
3. They like to have a workshop of their own—for their own age group. Some will not attend if they see there are younger kids (under age 12) in the class. It's not that they don't like the younger kids; it's just that they think the projects are too young for them. Remember that sixth graders think of themselves as tweens. This group will, however, teach younger kids how to create cool projects.
4. They like freedom and respect. They want guidelines, but they want to be able to create their own designs. They like to have their creations respected by group leaders and peers.

5. They want to be helpful. You will find that most teens are very helpful when it comes to distributing supplies, following the rules of the workshop, and helping to clean up.

6. They don't care to be compared to others. It's best not to have contests that put them into an art competition with one another. Everyone can create art. It's good to remind them that each person has his or her own style. Remind them of the many artists who were not mainstream in their art and ideas. We will normally find and study these artists in art history books.

7. They are smart and sensitive. They are willing to learn. They appreciate and enjoy the opportunity to create.

8. Most of all . . . they want to have fun!

Transform the Old—Celebrate the New

Going green doesn't mean reinventing the wheel. You already have many good program ideas in place, but they just need a little greening. Revamp the old and promote the new using environmentally friendly techniques.

Formats

Not all programs are the same, but some of the same elements are in all successful programs.

Before the Program

1. Plan it! Create a calendar of projects, events, and themes that reflect the environmental concerns and interests of your audience. Don't wait until Earth Day to offer a program celebrating the oceans, designing a fuel-free car, growing a garden, or breaking down and reusing a previously throwaway object into terrific jewelry.

2. Advertise it! Distribute press releases to local newspapers and other news outlets. Post it on Facebook, Twitter, and other blogs and Internet outlets. Make a book display that reflects the theme of the program.

3. Collect it! Create a recycling corner in your library that allows patrons to donate objects, papers, clothing, and so on for future use in programs. Give away any items that linger in the collection without use.

4. Rehearse it! Be sure to create projects beforehand. You will have more confidence in presenting the project and can head off any unforeseen challenges in making the piece.

5. Make it safe! Research the products that you are using. Visit the "Health & Safety Website" provided by the City of Tucson. You will be able to research the safety of a variety of art media. The website is located at http://www.tucsonaz.gov/arthaz ards/medium.html Read product labels for instructions regarding proper safety and disposal.

During the Program

1. Keep it safe! Make sure that your participants use safety goggles, gloves, and so on when appropriate during the program. When working with recycled objects, make sure that your teens are not handling lead cords, objects and papers with lead paints, and the like. A good overall reference for resources on artist's safety is *Keeping the Artist Safe: Resources about the Hazards of Arts and Crafts Material* at http://sis.nlm.nih. gov/enviro/arthazards.html#a1.

2. Localize it! As often as possible, buy from and support local grocers and other suppliers. You will have a fresher product and build goodwill with your neighbors. Invite local experts to speak at your programs and events. Invite local merchants to donate and attend events.

3. Keep them entertained! One way to stave off boredom and have a successful program is to provide something for all interests. Draw on those things that you know teens already like: food, music, and socializing. For example, if you are designing a program around a particular culture, include the cuisine, fashion, crafts, and sounds that reflect the life of that community. Use guest speakers as often as possible—to provide expert advice and bring an added zest to your program. Encourage social engagement through games and requesting volunteer participation. Don't hesitate to ask for help from your young patrons and others.

4. Document it! Take lots of photographs and videos (with permission, of course) so that you have a record and community memories of the event.

After the Program

1. Talk about it! Ask teens to give you substantive feedback—what went well, and how could the program have been improved? Offer incentives for filling out a survey. Ask teens for clarification so that you can improve. Keep a program journal, and incorporate the changes as soon as possible.

2. Share it! Ask teens to help you sort out the best of the photos and create a memory book; include it in your original display of the event. Follow up with another press release and postings on Internet websites and blogs.

3. Do it again! Be the librarian who is known for creating cool programming.

GREEN THEMES: WHERE DO YOU FIND THEM?

Where can you find resources for art projects and programming?

Search Them!

Search Green Words

Locate green art projects and green theme ideas using keywords in your Internet search.

---

green, going green, eco-friendly, repurposed, conservation, nature, green jobs, green crafts, green art, garden crafts, green teens, environmental, ecological, earth projects, green teen themes, green library programs, recycling

---

Searching the Stacks Online

The following are comprehensive resource starting points for anyone looking for programming themes and ideas.

Go Green Teens @ Carnegie Library of Pittsburgh. http://www.clpgh.org/teens/life/gogreen.cfm

Not only will you find a comprehensive list of books on the Carnegie online library search but the *Go Green* suggested links are very helpful since they are geared toward the teen population.

Teens—Princeton Public Library. http://www.princeton.lib.nj.us/teens/green/index.html

Not only does the Princeton library online resource have excellent resources of its own for teens, but it also gives a very helpful list of other green libraries' green teen programs.

Environment—Kalamazoo Public Library. http://www.kpl.gov/guides/environment/
Wow! The Kalamazoo library makes it easy for their patrons to be green. They provide
staff recommendations, hints for searching, databases, green magazines, local green
sources, and more.

Book It!

The following books will help you in developing themes and ideas for creating teen
programming in general.

Honnold, RoseMary. (2003). *101+ teen programs that work*. New York: Neal Schuman.
Anyone who is involved in teen programming on a regular basis knows this author's name.
This first book presents detailed ideas with follow-up comments from teens who participated in the
programs. There are many photographs that help us to understand the program and its success.

Honnold, R. (2005). *More teen programs that work*. New York: Neal Schuman.
This book of a follow-up to Honnold's first book and presents you with more teen programming
ideas, by Honnold and others. What makes her books so informative is that you know the author
has tried the programs and gives you the best. *More Teen Programs That Work* is worth the resources
alone.

Ott, Valerie A. (2006). *Teen programs with punch: A month by month guide*: Santa Barbara, CA: Libraries
Unlimited.
Ott's book is an outstanding reference for creating a calendar of events.

Pilger, Mary Ann. (1998). *Multicultural projects index: Things to make and do to celebrate festivals, cultures,
and holidays around the world*. New York: Libraries Unlimited.
Anyone interested in broadening their topic list will want this reference.

Seif, Marsha. (1997). *Reading programs for young adults: Complete plans for 50 theme-related units for public,
middle school, and high school libraries*. Jefferson, NC: McFarland.
Excellent resource for reading programs—good ideas and huge reference lists.

Going Digital!

Voice of Youth Advocates. http://www.voya.com
This is a must-have for those involved in teen programming. You will find teen booklists, reviews,
programming articles, advice, and more. It is a huge resource for young adult librarians.

3

◄❖►◄❖►◄❖►

MAKING IT TECHNO-GREEN: TECHIE SPACES, BLOGS, AND WEBSITES

All teens want their own space whether it's in the physical space of a library or virtually online. Learn ways to bring your library into the 21st century and share your programming ideas with your patrons.

A famous architect once said, "First we create our environment and then our environment creates us." Tweens and teens need a place where they can mingle, study, learn, create, and just hang out. It needs to be a place where enjoyable memories are made so that they want to return. Creating a cool environmental space for teens is a lot like creating an artwork. You will need a theme, a lot of imagination, and resources.

THE THEME

If you want to go green, the overriding theme of your teen space should demonstrate environmental awareness. It doesn't have to be a recycling or environmental theme. It can be a section on or display of oceans, whales, animals, endangered species, and so on. But be true to your green theme idea as you design your teen space. For instance, reuse plastics, heavy foam packaging, discarded newspapers and books, and other throwaway items to store and organize the space. Crates and cartons can also be repurposed to create shelving and displays. A visit to a garage sale or thrift store can produce a sofa, table, and other treasures that can be cleaned and restored through a little paint, helping the environment and your budget. Refresh old throw pillows by cleaning them and asking teens to paint them. You can use fabric paint to create interesting Matisse-inspired decorative pillows.

IMAGINATION

Let teens help you design the space by creating a collage of what the space should look like. What do they want in their space—books, a place to study, games, furniture, art prints, artwork? You can also create a preliminary layout or have a contest. Ask teens to

15

create a shoebox design of a teen space and place the boxes on display. Listen and gather feedback.

RESOURCES FOR GREEN SPACES

A good starting place is a thoughtful contemplation about teen spaces is the following book:

Farrelly, M.G. (2011). *Make room for teens!: Reflections on developing teen spaces in libraries*. Santa Barbara, CA: Libraries Unlimited.
>   There are not a lot of resources for developing teen spaces, but you don't need them when you have this book: It has plenty of advice and actual pictures to help.

Does your library space need a makeover? You will find examples and worksheets in this book:

Bolan, K. (2009). *Teen spaces: The step-by-step library makeover*. Chicago: American Library Association.
>   When it comes to buying materials for your collection, consider environmental friendly content in books, audiotapes, games, DVDs, magazines, and websites.

Here are a few examples:

Green Planet Films. http://www.greenplanetfilms.org/
>   Need a vendor that gives you eco-friendly choices? Here it is. You will find nature and environmental DVDs.

Sustainability-Themed Computer Games Come to the Classroom Edutopia. http://www.edutopia.org/environment-sustainability-computer-games
>   Imagine a computer game that includes environment responsibility into the design. It's here.

Websites, blogs, Facebook, podcasts, discussion groups, YouTube, UBroadcast, wikis, and more
>   Teens definitely want their own space and today it means virtual space. Imagine the possibilities of creating a network of environmental issue topics, projects, and artwork.

BraveNet.http://www.BraveNet.com
>   You will find free blogs, a message forum, a guestbook, a hit counter, e-mail forms, a mailing list, an online calendar, password protection, a photo album, chat rooms, web polls, speaking characters, e-cards, and more.

Doyle, M. (2007). *101+ great ideas for teen library web sites*. New York: Neal Schuman.
>   They know how to build and use a website. Do you? This book will help to catch you up.

Blogs

Teens Turning Green. http://www.teensturninggreen.org/index.php
>   Teens will find this blog very interesting for educating themselves about cosmetics and other products and for its networking possibilities.

Bloggers Blog. http://www.bloggersblog.com/teens/
>   This website outlines the use and importance of teens and blogging.

Create a zine: Your young adult patrons will think you are a super resource if you can tell them how to create a zine. This book will tell you what you need to know about creating a DIY magazine and/or comic, also known as a zine.

Todd, M., & Watson, E. (2006). *Whatcha mean, what's a zine? The art of making zines and minicomics*. Boston: Graphia Books.

Broadcast It!

You and your young adults can create your own radio station. Here's how:

About.com Radio. http://radio.about.com/od/createinternetradio/a/How-to-Create-Your-Own-Internet-Radio-Station_3.htm

Videotape It!

Your library can broadcast its own videos to the world. Think of the possibilities. It's easy. It is free at YouTube (http://www.youtube.com).

4

SHARING THE GREEN: MARKETING PROGRAMS AT YOUR HOME LIBRARY AND ON THE ROAD

How do you let others know about your programming ideas and encourage teens to spend even more time in the library?

CREATE A CLUB

Art Club

Connect with local middle and high school teachers and principals. Suggest that space in your library be used as a place where teens can meet to learn more about art, visit local galleries and art museums, develop art skills, and meet local artists. Your will need an art advisor unless you have your own hidden art talents that you wish to share. Ask students to help you select art history prints for your library collection. Invite artists to exhibit their work and let teens help to arrange and sponsor the event.

Ecology Club

Volunteer Them

You already know that your teens and tweens are socially concerned. They have volunteered for your teen advisory committees, have participated in arts and crafts and story-time activities for younger children, provided you with a list of suggested summer reading, and suggested the henna tattooing program that was offered at your branch last year. You appreciate their input, but did you know that you can encourage them to get funding for creating their own unique volunteer project? Teens can apply for a $500 grant for doing something good such as helping the environment, fighting diabetes or poverty, or making their neighborhood a better place to live. You can create a program centered around volunteerism and give them advice and support for creating their own volunteer project. See details for funding and project ideas at www.Dosomething.org. The organization also strongly promotes teen clubs and offers a grant application for teens creating a teen action club. What a better place to hold a "Do Something" meeting than *your* library.

The website outlines what projects other teens are involved in and gives them ideas for creating their own projects. It's a perfect way for teens to find causes and network with like-minded others. Although no adults are required to run the meetings and projects, imagine offering a program that centers around volunteerism and letting students know that you are a good resource.

HOW TO START A LIBRARY CLUB

This website will give you practical advice for starting a library club:

http://thelibraryclub.wordpress.com/2007/10/30/start-a-library-club/

Display it. Exhibit it. Create in-your-face, popping-off-the-wall environmental displays that you can use to motivate reading, ecology, and art programs. After they have created it, it's time to exhibit it. This is one of the best ways to showcase art and involve teens.

Display It!

Displays need a theme, and they need something that attracts the eye, mind, and heart. But first you need an idea. You can use book themes, an upcoming program idea, summer reading programs, or subject topics:

Recycling Plastics	Paper boxes	Fast Food Containers	Fashions	
The Environment	Endangered Species	Water Sheds	Volunteerism	Social Issues
The Oceans	Whales, Dolphins, Walrus	Tigers	Gulf Coast	Birds and Environment

It's not just the theme but what you use to create it that matters.

| Vacations | Where in the World | At the Beach | Summer Careers | Jobs for Environmentalists |

Carbon Footprint Display

Create five large footprints or order the giant flip-flop papers from Oriental Trading Company (http://www.orientaltrading.com). Under each category write the five areas of concern outlined on the Zero Footprint for Kids website (http://www.zerofootprintkids.com/kids_home.aspx): transportation, what you eat, home and school, what you use, and what you throw away. Create a handout outlining the name of the website and instructions for calculating your carbon footprint. Bring in books, DVDs, magazines, and other information that helps teens figure out how to lower their carbon footprints.

Plastic Bottle Fountain

Create a centerpiece that they will talk about for a long time. Design a teen plastic bottle fountain by placing empty water bottles together to form a body. Use plastic tubing and follow the manufacturer's instruction to create a teen recycled water fountain. Use red Kool-Aid for the blood (the water that runs through the tubing).

Figure 4–1: Form shape

Figure 4–2: Add tubing

Figure 4–3: Place motor

Figure 4–4: Plastic fountain exhibit

NOTES

_____

_____

_____

_____

_____

Exhibit It!

The library is an excellent place to exhibit your group's artwork and let them learn about local art professionals. San Diego's Library Visual Arts Program is so successful that there is a library art curator who schedules and organizes professional art shows throughout the year. There are many areas that are available for exhibits in the library. Cases, walls, corners, designated areas, entrance ways, and courtyards all make good locations for exhibiting artwork.

There are also opportunities in the neighborhood that provide a place for teens to show their work and a way for you to market your library art programs. Grocery stores, real estate agencies, retail clothing stores, banks, churches, senior centers, coffeehouses, and restaurants are places where art is often welcome. Both businesses/organizations and libraries benefit from the mutual arrangement. Create art projects that involve putting art on the walls and bringing handmade greeting cards to those living in senior facilities.

High and middle schools—private, public, and charter—are important resources for the young adult librarian. Teachers, principals, and library personnel can help you market your programs, give you ideas, and provide space to show teen art projects created at your library.

Go Virtual!

There are many online art galleries and organizations that welcome submissions of artwork by children, teens, and adults. You can also upload art to your website and blog sites.

Teen Ink. http://www.teenink.com/?do=showlogin
    This website offers online writing resources and more for teens. It offers teens a chance to publish, exhibit their artwork, take classes, and network.

Promote It, and They Will Come

No one likes to have a party where no one shows up. That's how it feels sometimes when you are offering teen programming. You may have the best programming in town, but if teens don't know about it, they won't show up.

Here are a few tips that you might not have thought about for getting the news out.

1. **Tell their parents** and other adults. Don't rely on young adult mailing lists. Use the librarian's library list and ask the adults to tell friends and relatives about the special guest speaker, art program, or other special event.
2. **Take it to the movies.** Ask your local theater if you can get a reduced-cost or free advertising rate and post a short announcement on the slideshow before the movie. Be one of the coming attractions.
3. **It's on cable.** Most cable stations have a public relations station that allows free advertising of your program or, better yet, create a public access commercial. Your cable company may be required to provide free commercial airtime advertising.
4. **Play it** on the radio. Ask local radio stations for airtime. Be sure to promote the announcement on popular teen stations and their parents' stations.
5. **Tell the teacher** and principal too. Talk to the teachers and principals of the local middle and high schools, and ask them to make the announcement over the intercom or closed circuit television if possible.
6. **Make them an offer they can't refuse.** Have a pizza night, contest, or other special guest speaker that would be of interest to a teen who normally wouldn't visit the library. Give teens a special 2 Fer (2 for 1) Prize for bringing in a partner to an event.
7. **Invite an expert.** An artist, author, sports star, or other interesting guest will have their own publicity machine. Your press release to the local paper and local news will get the attention of the editors more easily.

8. **Create an art exhibition and contest.** Invite local artists to compete in a "recycled" art exhibition. The City of Encinitas Library overlooking the ocean near San Diego just held its second annual exhibition and had an opening reception and contest for the winning artists. Ask the winning artist to offer a workshop for teens.

9. **Use the technology.** Remember to advertise the event in the local newspapers, on library iPods, and on the Internet, especially on social networking sites like Facebook. There are also many local entertaining and news sites that allow event listings.

PART II

ART PROGRAMS AND PROJECTS

5

SIMPLY INEXPENSIVE ONE HOUR ECO-FRIENDLY ART PROGRAMS

Creative programming doesn't have to be expensive. This chapter includes simple-to-create, fast, budget-wise, and effective programming ideas that teach participants about the environment.

PROJECT LIST

Fabulous Paper Fashion

Recycled Cars

Sassy Grassy Grass Portraits

Music Box (from a recycled book)

Dancers Paper Style

Camouflage Carry Catch All

FABULOUS PAPER FASHION

Teens love to create fashions. This program uses recycled materials to create fun fashions from everyday materials that you already have and a few found objects and bits and pieces. All you need to add is lots of imagination.

Program Suggestions

Sponsor a fashion design day at your library. Create a Fashion Show. Hold a Career Day. Invite a designer to your library to judge the designs.

What You Will Need

Roll of brown paper or newspaper

Tacky glue

Duct tape

Scissors

Measuring tape

Found objects: ribbons, buttons, bottle caps, recycled belt, plastic bottle for stencil decoration

Step-by-Step Instructions

1. Roll out brown paper or newspaper.
2. Fold in half lengthwise.
3. Cut a circle at the top of the paper. Open it. That's your neckline.
4. Find the middle of the circle and cut lengthwise to "open" the collar. Glue the sides together, leaving openings for arms. To make a dress, leave full length; for a shirt, cut to the preferred length.
5. Decorate with duct tape and bits and pieces. Cut fringe to make the brown paper look like leather. The bottom of a plastic bottle is used to stencil the dress. Use a bottle top to create the center of a flower.

Want the brown paper to look like faux leather? Before you begin working with it, crumple, rub, and distress it. The harder you work, the more like leather it will look. It's ok if it tears—that makes it look more authentic.

Encourage teens to create the most outrageous designs. These designs are not to wear but are art to be shown in an art exhibit or display.

Gr. 8–12

$$ out of $$$$$

Tie It to the Technology!

Professional Resources

E-How: How to Host a Runway Fashion Show for Teens. http://www.ehow.com/how_2253558_host-runway-fashion-show-teens.html

    You will find general tips for organizing a fashion show for teens that you can use in a library setting.

The Paper Dress—History of a Ready to Tear Invention. http://inventorspot.com/articles/history_paper_11174

    You probably were a young person or not yet born when the paper dress was first introduced in the mid-1960s. Read guest blogger Samantha Marcelo's article at *Inventorspot*. The article will give you interesting and fun facts that you can share with your teen groups.

Teen Alternative Fashion Show: Voya MVT Program on Vimeo. http://vimeo.com/6725515

    Watch this award-winning fashion show at the Fayetteville Public Library in Fayetteville, Arkansas.

Resources for Young Adults

Grandon, Adrian. *200 projects to get you into fashion design*. Hauppauge, NY: Barrons Educational Series.

    This highly illustrated book gives fashion wannabes a lot to look at and think about. It also provides young adults with practical advice that they can use to make career choices.

Teen Vogue. (2009). *The teen vogue handbook: An insider's guide to careers in fashion*. New York: Razorbill.

    The *Teen Vogue Handbook* is an exciting addition to a teen collection. Teens will find interviews and get a peek into the possibility of a career in the fashion industry.

Magazines and Periodicals

Teen Vogue Magazine. Conde Nast Publications.

    You will find this classic teen fashion magazine online at http://www.teenvogue.com

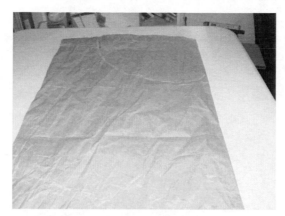

Figure 5–1: Design layout

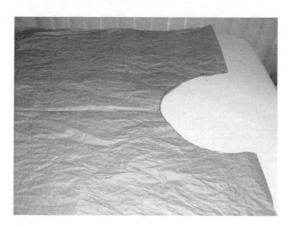

Figure 5–2: Cut the design

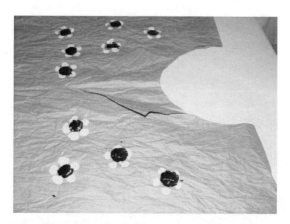

Figure 5–3: Embellish it

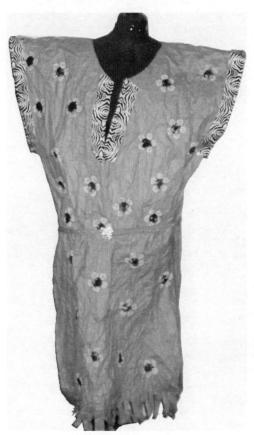

Figure 5–4: Nonwearable decorative paper dress

NOTES

_____

_____

_____

_____

_____

SASSY GRASSY GRASS PORTRAITS

This too-cute portrait sculpture teaches teens about growing things, recycling, and art.

Program Suggestions

Earth Day. Group Garden. Gift Giving. Ecological Fairs. Sadie Hawkins Day. Fund-raising.

What You Will Need

Nylon footies (you can order these through retail supply stores or use discarded nylon stockings)
Soil
Cat grass seeds or other fast-growing seeds
Tacky glue (Aleene's)
Peat pots
Craft items such as plastic eyes, soft foam, and recycled fabrics

Step-by-Step Instructions

1. Fill bottom of nylon footie with several grass seeds (minimum of six).
2. Cover the seeds in the nylon footie with soil. The dirt should fill the sock about halfway and make a round ball of soil.
3. Water the soil so that it is wet, but do not overly water it.
4. Place filled nylon footie into a paper planter (the peat pot) 3 inches high by 3 inches wide. Place footie in container so that the seed side is turned up facing sunlight.
5. Water daily. Within a few days you will see green blades poking through the nylon. It will take another week or so for the grass to be ready for decoration.
6. Decorate the paper planter and the nylon footie with craft materials. Continue to water the grass, and move to a larger container as it grows.

Teaching Tips

Keep portrait head in the sun.
Water using spray bottle.
You may need to poke a hole in the nylon and pull grass through it.

Gr. 6–9
$$ out of $$$$$

Tie It to the Technology!

Professional Resources

Armstrong Garden Center. http://www.armstronggarden.com/
    This online and on-site nursery offers many resources for beginning gardeners.

Garden Guides. http://www.gardenguides.com/85040-make-plant-pots-newspapers.html
    This guide outlines how you can make plant pot starters out of newspapers.

Resources for Young Adults

Kingsolver, B., Kingsolver, C., & Hopp S. (2008). *Animal, vegetable, miracle: A year of food life*. New York: Harper Perennial.
    Imagine eating locally and even growing your own food. What would you learn from your experience? This highly recommended book presents a firsthand account of looking at food in a new way.

Watch a Grass Head Growing on YouTube. http://www.youtube.com/watch?v=FsJjEkLUZMI
    Everyone will enjoy watching the time-lapse growth and adventure of this grass head.

Figure 5–5: Plant

Figure 5–6: Grow

Figure 5–7: Decorate

Figure 5–8: Sassy grassy portrait

NOTES

_____

_____

_____

_____

_____

DANCERS PAPER STYLE

Create artwork with a dance theme using recycled paper.

Program Suggestions

Recycled paper-art "dancers" can be used as part of a Dance@the Library program. Invite a dance teacher to teach teens the waltz, tango, salsa, and swing dances. Sponsor a formal party that shows off their skills. Have a dance-a-thon at the library.

What You Will Need

Paint

brushes

glue

construction paper or poster board

various papers such as painted magazine pages, junk mail, painted paper bags, scraps of gift wrap, and other recycled papers

Step-by-Step Instructions

1. Begin by painting various sheets of discarded paper such as magazines, junk mail, paper bags, and so on. Let dry.
2. Tear papers into basic shapes (squares, circles, triangles) and irregular abstract shapes, along with long, short, and varied shapes.
3. Play with the shapes to create a figure or abstract.
4. Glue pieces onto a piece of construction paper or poster board.

Teaching Tips

Encourage teens to bring their own toss-away scraps.

Let paint dry and then tear.

Don't bother to paint papers that have color or texture.

Be creative in the tearing process.

Tear on curves and angles to create motion.

Gr. 7–12

$ out of $$$$$

Tie It to the Technology!

Professional Resources

How to Tear Paper. YouTube. http://www.youtube.com/watch?v=QmaE89_qHnk
    This Scrapbook T.V. presentation shares hints concerning working with paper.

An Overview of Dance Styles, Teen Dance, SAPL's Resource Guides at San Antonio Public Library. http://guides.mysapl.org/teendance
    This library website is a good resource for books and dance terms for that library's own patrons and other librarians.

Resources for Young Adults

Dance Help. http://www.dancehelp.com/articles/dance-events/dance-movies.aspx
    This is a good resource for locating information about old and new dance movies on DVD. Teens will find articles, tips, forums, and other things related to dance.

Glee Television Series (Fox). http://www.fox.com/glee/
    All things Glee. Episodes and resources and more.

Sonnenblick, J. (2006). *Drums, girls and dangerous pie*. New York: Scholastic Paperbacks.
    Teens will enjoy this tale of a 13-year-old boy, Steven, who immerses himself in his music when life brings the unexpected challenges of a brother diagnosed with cancer and other family and personal pressures.

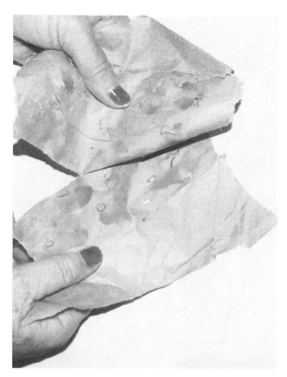

Figure 5–9: Tear

Figure 5–10: Arrange

Figure 5–11: Glue

Figure 5–12: Dancers paper style

NOTES

_____

_____

_____

_____

_____

RECYCLED CARS

The interest in recyclables and ecological substitutes for fossil fuels will be one of the most important environmental challenges of car designers and engineers in the 21st century. This project focuses on design aspects of futuristic car design. Teens will use recyclables such as magazines, newspapers, packaging, old toys, and other toss-aways to create unique recycled art cars.

Program Suggestions

Teen Art Program. Earth Day. Science and Engineering Research. Design a New Car. Cars and the Future. Cars without Fossil Fuels Design Competition.

Recycled cars can be used as a display, an art program, an Earth Day program, or a library promotional contest.

What You Will Need

Hobby store plastic mold or cardboard car template (shoeboxes, packaging materials, and other items may be used as the initial mold)

newspapers or magazines, Aleene's Tacky Glue

papier-mâché

paint and brushes

recycled objects

Step-by-Step Instructions

Workshop #1

1. Distribute plastic mold.
2. Oil the inside of the mold so that the papier-mâché will be easily released.
3. Tear newspaper or magazine pages into small strips.
4. Make a papier-mâché paste from flour and water. It should be the consistency of cake batter or medium-thick glue.
5. Cover the inside of the mold with two layers of newspaper or magazine strips that have been dipped into the paste.
6. Let it dry.

Workshop #2

1. Carefully release papier-mâché from the mold and add accessories using found objects and paint.

Teaching Tips

Discuss the importance of innovative car designs as they relate to cars of the future. Show examples of hybrid and other alternative-fuel cars.

Create an example to share with the group.

You can find plastic molds for this project at your local hobby store.

Variations

Create a group electric, solar, or water-powered model car.

Gr. 7–12

$$$ out of $$$$$

Tie It to the Technology!

Professional Resources

Car Talk. http://www.cartalk.com/

If you have ever listened to the hosts Tom and Ray on PBS's *Car Talk,* you will know why this is a good place to start for anyone needing a reason to love and understand cars.

Sports Car Designer Software. http://www.sportscardesigner.com/
   Imagine designing your own car like the professionals do it. You will enjoy it as much as your young adult audience.

Resources for Young Adults

Leitman, S. (2009). *Build your own plug-in hybrid electric vehicle*. New York: McGraw-Hill TAB Electronics.
   This highly popular book will explain to teens what it means to go from oil to electricity. Don't expect them to build a hybrid but to understand the process after reading this book.

McCarthy, T. (2007). *Auto mania: Cars, consumers, and the environment*. New Haven, CT: Yale University Press.
   This book explores Americans' love for the automobile and the changes this beloved machine has gone through over the years.

Vaitheeswaran, V., & Carson, I. (2008). *ZOOM: The global race to fuel the car of the future*. New York: Twelve.
   Teens interested in politics and American ingenuity will find this an interesting read.

Figure 5–13: Mold

Figure 5–14: Remove

Figure 5–15: Embellish

Figure 5–16: Recycled cars

NOTES

_____

_____

_____

_____

_____

MUSIC BOX (FROM A RECYCLED BOOK)

It's a hard fact to accept, but each year many books end up in landfills because they are outdated, have not sold at book sales, or have not been or apparently can't be given away. In some cases, they are in poor condition. Artists and designers have started to use books to create art projects and even furniture. This project reintroduces a book as a music box.

Program Suggestions

Music Appreciation Day at the Library. Re-Introduce It! Teens Re-create Objects for a New Purpose Program. Earth Day Celebration. Celebration of Thomas Edison.

What You Will Need

Recycled books (hardbacks work best)
Acrylic paint in various colors and paint brushes
Box cutters
Aleene's Tacky Glue
Optional: Musical movement components. See resources for where to purchase.

Step-by-Step Instructions

1. Lay book flat, and open book at center.
2. Cut a square about one inch deep.
3. Glue, paint, and decorate book (see photo illustrations).
4. Optional musical movement component can be placed at the bottom of the book, on the back of the book, or inside the cover and fastened according to the manufacturer's directions.

Teaching Tips

Present the history of musical boxes (see Chapius's book) with a display of books and DVDs.

Gr. 8–12
$$$$ out of $$$$$

Tie It to the Technology!
Professional Resources

Chapuis, A. (1980). *History of the musical box and of mechanical music*. Springfield, MO: Music Box Society.
Klock it! http://www.klockit.com
> You will be able to find musical movement components at this website.

Mechanical Music Digest. http://www.mmdigest.com/index.html
> Variety of resources for resources and vendors.

Resources for Young Adults

Carl Hiaasen. http://www.carlhiaasen.com/index.shtml
> You've read *Hoot* and *Flush* from this teen environmental writer. What else is he up to currently?

Discover Mechanical or Automated Music on the Internet. http://www.musicamecanica.org/musica_mecanica/index.html
> Many resources for listening to musical postcards and mechanical music and museums around the world.

Swinburne, Stephen R. (1998). *In good hands: Behind the scenes at a center for orphaned and injured birds*. San Francisco: Sierra Club Books.
> Although designed for younger readers, teens will also enjoy this highly illustrative book that stars Hannah, a 16-year-old girl who gains invaluable life and learning experience at her volunteer position at the Vermont Raptor Center.

Figure 5–17: Layout of book

Figure 5–18: Paint and cut

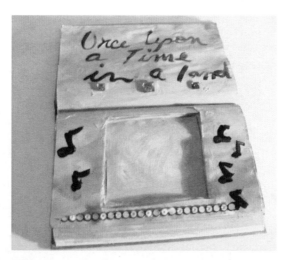

Figure 5–19: Decorate

Figure 5–20: Music box

NOTES

_____

_____

_____

_____

_____

CAMOUFLAGE CATCH ALL

Your teen groups will like this masculine-friendly art project that helps them organize important items like CDs, DVDs, and other valuables.

Program Suggestions

Earth Day. Gift Giving. Ecological Fairs. Projects for Boys.

What You Will Need

Two ring carriers from six- or eight-packs of soda or water with handles intact

Pencil

Old T-shirt (preferably green or khaki color)

White chalk and yardstick or measuring tape

Scissors and Aleene's Tacky Glue

Glue gun and glue sticks

Six to eight pieces of white fabric and six to eight pieces cardboard (the kind of packaging that is inserted into a new shirt, for instance), all large enough to fit the inside of the plastic rings of the plastic soda ring carriers

Green, brown, white, and black fabric paint, and a round brush.

Step-by-Step Instructions

1. Lay the T-shirt out with arms extending outward. Draw a line using chalk and yardstick from under one arm to the other. Cut with scissors.
2. Fold the bottom of the T-shirt under one inch and glue the bottom of the T-shirt together using Aleene's Tacky Glue.
3. Using a pencil and the plastic rings as a guide, measure and trace a circle onto the fabric and cardboard and cut.
4. Paint the fabric creating camouflage designs using the fabric paints. Encourage teens to add white to lighten colors or a small amount of black to darken them. Let dry.
5. Glue fabric into plastic carrier circles and then place and glue cardboard on the back of the fabric circles. Let dry.
6. Place one soda ring carrier handle in the center of the top of the T-shirt and glue using glue gun. Let dry. Glue the second soda carrier handle to the top of the T-shirt. Let dry.

Teaching Tips

To make the tote more girl-friendly, use different fabric and paint.

Gr. 6–9

$$$ out of $$$$$

Tie It to the Technology!

Professional Resources

How Stuff Works (Discovery Channel). How Animals Use Camouflage. http://animals.howstuffworks.com/animal-facts/11-animals-that-use-camouflage.htm
   This very interesting website will help you explain how animals use camouflage to protect themselves.

Wikipedia. Camouflage Patterns. http://en.wikipedia.org/wiki/List_of_camouflage_patterns
   This is a good resource for learning about and sharing information about camouflage patterns found around the world very interesting.

Resources for Young Adults

Fashion Encyclopedia: Stephen Sprouse. http://www.fashionencyclopedia.com/Sp-To/Sprouse-Stephen.html
   This fashion designer/artist is known for creating camouflage clothing, among other designs.

The Warhol: Resources and Lessons—Camouflage: Sound Activity. http://edu.warhol.org/aract_camo.html
   Teens will enjoy reading about the pop artist Andy Warhol and completing this camouflage exercise from this website dedicated to this late artist.

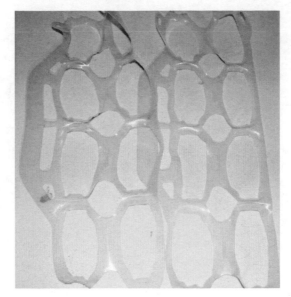

Figure 5–21: Plastic ring handle

Figure 5–22: T-shirt

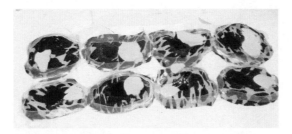

Figure 5–23: Decorate rings

Figure 5–24: Camouflage catch all

NOTES

_____

_____

_____

_____

_____

6

FAST-FOOD CONTAINERS AND OTHER TOSS-AWAYS

Don't throw away those fast-food containers and other toss-aways. Take them from the trash can to the treasure chest. The programs are 45 minutes in length unless otherwise noted.

PROJECT LIST	
After Juice Aftershave	Eat It! Paint It!
Drink It and Grow It: Plant It in the Library	Gumball or Candy Machine Replica

AFTER JUICE AFTERSHAVE

A fast-food apple juice container is used to hold aftershave.

Program Suggestions

This project makes a good gift for Father's Day. Recycling. Earth Day. Product Design.

What You Will Need

Full sheet of print-and-peel sheets.

Printable labels, http://www.vintageimagecraft.com/after-shave-bottle.html

Digital image and paint program

Empty fast-food bottle

Natural aftershave recipe, such as About.com Frugal Living aftershave recipe, http://frugalliving.about.com/od/beautyhealthcare/qt/After_Shave.htm

Step-by-Step Instructions

1. Create the label using the digital image and paint program. Use adhesive print paper.
2. Make and pour aftershave into bottle.

Teaching Tips

Encourage teens to create their own labels and print them. Also, help your group create a short commercial "selling" their aftershave. Be sure all get a chance to "star" with their design in the video.

Tie It to the Technology!

Professional Resources

Gaines, Thom. (2010). *Digital photo madness! 50 weird and wacky things to do with your digital camera*. Ashville, NC: Lark Books.
    This book gives teens important basics of digital technology and skill combined with fun project ideas.

Various papers for printing. Office Depot website. http://www.officedepot.com

Resources for Young Adults

Campbell, M., & Long, D. (2006). *Digital photography for teens*. Florence, KY: Course Technology.
    This is a serious technical how-to book for teens.

Hampe, B. (1998). *Making videos for money: Planning and producing information videos, commercials, and infomercials*. Austin: Holt Paperbacks.

Styr, C., & Waken, M. (2009). *Click: The ultimate photography guide for generation now*. New York: Amphoto.
    This is one for the young audience stacks. Written by an 18-year-old, this photography book presents many ideas for subject matter and the artist's perspective. It's worth the chapter on nature and landscape photography alone.

Figure 6–1: Design

Figure 6–2: Pour

Figure 6–3: Package

Figure 6–4: After juice aftershave

NOTES

_____

_____

_____

_____

_____

DRINK IT AND GROW IT: PLANT IT IN THE LIBRARY

Use fast-food drinking cups to start seedlings, and then plant them to make a library garden.

Program Suggestions

Build a library garden in the courtyard or inside the library and watch the plants grow. May Day. Garden Days. Environmental Design.

What You Will Need

Fast-food cups

Potting soil

Cat grass seeds or other fast-growing plants such as popcorn, salad bowl lettuce, and flowers such as marigolds, sunflowers, and others

For plant sticks (to identify seedlings): craft sticks, school glue, disposable heavyweight paper, and a variety of colored markers

Fast-food recycled plastic bowls and trays (request and collect these)

Step-by-Step Instructions

1. Ask teens to save and bring their fast-food containers to the library.
2. Instruct teens to cut cups into 4-inch seedling cups and add soil.
3. Pour soil into cup, and plant flower or plant seeds. Plant small seeds in shallow soil and lightly water. Use more seeds than you expect to grow so that your group won't be disappointed if some of the seeds don't germinate. Bring extra cups and plant your own seedlings to replace those of participants that don't grow.
4. Ask teens to create unique plant/flower plant sticks using the preceding materials. Stick the planters into the cup.
5. Place in sun. As the plants grow, transfer them into recyclable plastic bowls. Poke holes in the bottom of the plastic containers. Use a second recycled plastic tray or bowl to contain the water that may spill out of the plastic bowl.

Gr. 6–12

$$ out of $$$$$

Tie It to the Technology!

Professional Resources

Grant, T., & Littlejohn, G. (eds.). (2001). *Greening school grounds: Creating habitats for learning*. Toronto: Green Teacher.
> This book shows how to green school spaces by creating gardens and other environmental projects in place of the traditional school yard.

Green Teacher magazine, P.O. Box 1431, Lewiston, NY 14092 (http://www.greenteacher.com)
> Very good resource for classroom teachers interested in greening and teaching environmental subjects. This magazine would be helpful to librarians working with all grade levels including teenage groups.

Weaver, Stephanie. (2007). *Creating great visitor experiences: A guide for museums, parks, zoos, gardens, and libraries*. Walnut Creek, CA: Left Coast.
> This is an interesting book that uses the model of the nonprofit to communicate how to make an institution such as a library welcoming and accessible to the public.

Resources for Young Adults

Edible School Yard. http://www.edibleschoolyard.org/
> An interesting website that includes a video that explains this unique school program using gardening and cooking as an integral part of the program at the Martin Luther King Middle School in California.

National Garden Association. http://www.garden.org/home
> Teens who are interested in gardening and how things grow will appreciate this excellent resource with interesting educational materials.

Solomon, S. (2006). *Gardening when it counts: Growing food in hard times*. Gabriola Island, BC: New Society.
> Teens will enjoy the concept of this book written by a master gardener who has taught at the University of Oregon.

Figure 6–5: Plant

Figure 6–6: Grow

Figure 6–7: Garden

54

Figure 6–8: Library garden

NOTES

_____

_____

_____

_____

_____

EAT IT! PAINT IT!

Teens will enjoy the unique Renaissance artist Giuseppe Arcimboldo, who used food to create surreal portraits. You will have fun watching them make their own unique artwork out of fast-food salads.

Program Suggestions

Be Healthy@the Library. Happy Birthday Arcimboldo! Art History.

What You Will Need

Fast-food salad and bowl
A variety of floral picks and wire (at least five per teen) to use to attach food if necessary
Digital camera

Step-by-Step Instructions

1. Visit the website for Renaissance-era artist Giuseppe Arcimboldo at http://www.giuseppe-arcimboldo.org/ to become acquainted with this artist's work and share this resource with your group. Create a display of his work prior to the program.
2. Keep things clean. You will need a clean long table covered with a cloth. Ask students to wash hands before handling salad so that they can eat the salad after the art project is complete. Provide individual white placemats for a backdrop.
3. Encourage teens to "play" with the salad contents: to try numerous ways of arranging the ingredients to create innovative portraits in the style of Arcimboldo. As teens look through the Arcimboldo photos, they will find that he even at times uses the salad bowl effectively in his work.
4. Make it digital. Take pictures of the various portraits.

Teaching Tips

Print photos and hang them in the display you have created for this program.
Share photos on your library blog or website along with images of teens enjoying themselves.

Gr. 6–12
$$ out of $$$$$

Tie It to the Technology!

Professional Resources

Giuseppe Arcimboldo
> You will find many good image sources for looking at this artist when you perform a Google Image search. Type in Google Search-Images-Giuseppe Arcimboldo.

Help Guide Website: Healthy Fast Food-Tips for Making Healthier Fast Food Choice. http://helpguide.org/life/fast_food_nutrition.htm
> Let's face it, teens and adults like to eat out. This article will help you show teens how they can make healthier choices when it comes to what they buy on the go.

Resources for Young Adults

DaCosta, T. (2009). *Arcimboldo: Visual jokes, natural history, and still-life painting*. Chicago: University of Chicago Press.
> Highly illustrated with background information about the artist.

Kunsthistorisches Museum. http://www.khm.at/en/kunsthistorisches-museum/the-museum/
> Take your teens on a virtual trip to this museum near Vienna and see Arcimboldo's work and the work of other artists who were contemporaries with him. Be sure to click English.

The National Gallery of Art. "Art of Arcimboldo 1526–1593 Nature and Fantasy." National Gallery of Art, brochure accompanying exhibition, September 19, 2010–January 9, 2011
> This brochure presents easy-to-understand material about this artist and gives an up-close and personal view of him.

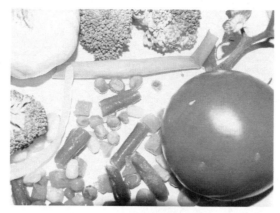

Figure 6–9: Assemble vegetables

Figure 6–10: Play with your food

Figure 6–11: Make a face

Figure 6–12: Giuseppe Arcimboldo–inspired artwork

NOTES

_____

_____

_____

_____

_____

GUMBALL OR CANDY MACHINE REPLICA

Teens can create their own small version of a gumball, candy, or other treat machine using recycled plastic cups and other recyclables from a local store or the food court of their favorite mall.

Program Suggestions

Recycling. Valentine's Day. Retro Days. Back to the '50s.

What You Will Need

One eight-ounce plastic drinking cup and an empty eight-ounce yogurt container. The squat-type drinking cups that are wide and short work the best. The bottoms of both containers should be the same size.

A lid that will fit easily on the plastic drinking cup (a plastic lid from another container will work better than the original lid)

Black acrylic paint and brushes to paint the yogurt container

Glue (tacky glue or glue sticks used with a glue gun)

For the accessories, a bottle cap, and a small piece of cardboard and markers or paint (black and red) to create the machine slot

Gumballs, jelly beans, peanuts, or other treats

Step-by-Step Instructions

1. Paint the outside of the bottom container or cup.
2. Let dry.
3. Turn upside down.
4. Place clear container on top of black container and glue.
5. Fill with candy.
6. Paint lid and bottle cap.
7. Place painted lid with bottle top on the top of the lid.
8. Place cardboard coin slot onto black container, and add embellishment to the top of the lid with black paint.

Teaching Tips

Be sure that paint is fully dry before placing the black container on the clear container.

Gr. 6–9
$$ out of $$$$$

Tie It to the Technology!

Professional Resources

E-How: How to Make Gumballs. http://www.ehow.com/how_4923458_make-gumballs.html
Teens can make their own gumballs, or you can bring them for them.

Oriental Trading Company. http://www.orientaltrading.com
You can buy bulk candy at this online craft supply store. Visit and rent a pinball for your library.

Pacific Pinball Museum. http://pacificpinball.org/home
See the history, art, and technology of pinball machines at this website. This pinball museum is in San Francisco, but you may have a pinball museum near you. Do some research and see if there is a pinball museum in your area.

Young Adult Resources

About.Com: The History of Pinball and Pinball Machines. http://inventors.about.com/od/pstartinventions/a/pinball.htm
Often, where you find pinball machines you will find coin-operated gumball machines. Teens can read about the history of pinball machines, along with learning the technical names of parts, on this website.

Figure 6–13: Paint containers

Figure 6–14: Glue containers

Figure 6–15: Accessorize

Figure 6–16: Gumball and candy machine replica

NOTES

_____

_____

_____

_____

_____

7

GREEN THEMES FOR A GREENBACK: ART PROJECTS FOR UNDER $1.00

These projects are perfect for "make it and take it" and a variety of programs for libraries on a budget. Complete each project for under $1.00. Projects take one hour unless otherwise specified.

PROJECT LIST

Desktop Organizer with Fake Spill	Let's Get Physical: Weights
Way Cool Bark Jewelry	Your State Bird

DESKTOP ORGANIZER WITH FAKE SPILL

This project involves creating a desktop organizer made of recycled materials (a frozen food container, box lid, and plastic cup). Teens learn simple techniques for creating a desktop organizer.

Program Suggestions

A Day at the Office. Finding a Job. Writing Resumes.

What You Will Need

A variety of recycled materials such as cardboard food packages, plastic cups, and fast-food containers.

A box lid from a storage box for the tray.

A variety of paint and brushes

Brown paint and school glue for faux coffee or soda, as well as tacky glue to adhere objects

Step-by-Step Instructions

1. Cut an opening in the cardboard box lid large enough to place one or more of the recycled containers into a secured slot. Cautionary note: Use care with box cutters.
2. Wash and dry all the recycled containers you have collected. You can also glue the containers onto the cardboard box lid.
3. Make a fake spill by mixing brown paint with glue. Let dry. It may take a couple of days for the glue to dry completely.

Gr. 8–10
$ out of $$$$$

Tie It to the Technology!

Professional Resources

Ecobo: Ten Clever Furniture Designs from Recycled Materials. http://ecoble.com/2008/05/28/ten-clever-furniture-designs-from-recycled-materials/
  You and your young adult group will enjoy looking at these unique designs created from recycled materials. Use this website exhibit as inspiration for your own projects.

Resources for Young Adults

About.Com: Teen Job Search Guide. http://jobsearch.about.com/od/teenstudentgrad/a/teenjobcenter.htm
  This website provides basic job-hunting advice tips and resources including search and interview techniques.

Brea, Abbie. Pursue your passions. Teen Ink. http://www.teenink.com/college_guide/college_articles/article/92530/Pursue-Your-Passions/
  Teen Ink provides a space for teens to publish their work and discuss it. There are also networking possibilities and other resources for this age group. This article discusses the career of journalism and decisions involved in making life choices.

Figure 7–1: Locate objects

Figure 7–2: Cut openings

Figure 7–3: Paint and glue

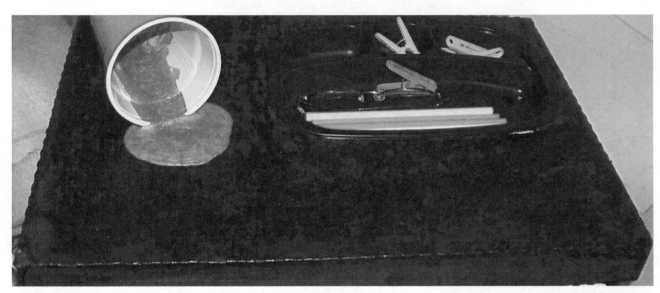

Figure 7–4: Desk organizer with fake spill

NOTES

_____

_____

_____

_____

_____

WAY COOL BARK JEWELRY

Bark normally falls in autumn, but in California I've seen it on the ground in the spring. Nature has beautiful natural treasures to use in your art projects. Take your teens on a field trip to a local natural setting to discover eucalyptus or natural bark common to your area that has fallen on the ground. (Note: Instruct teens not to peel bark from a tree.) You can also gather it yourself prior to the workshop. Use it to create unique jewelry pieces.

Program Suggestions

Earth Day. Mother's Day. Arbor Day. Native American Celebration. Ecological Fair. Fund-Raising. Jewelry Making.

What Will You Need

Cardboard for earring shapes and backing

Earring posts or clips, bark

Brown postal paper or paper bag paper

Embellishments (feathers, beads, sticks)

Tacky glue

Scissors

Step-by-Step Instructions

1. Cut a piece of cardboard into a simple geometric shape, such as a square, circle, or triangle.
2. Place bark over cardboard.
3. Add feathers or other embellishments.
4. Attach earring studs by applying tacky glue.

Teaching Tips

Be sure bark is not gathered from a protected environment such as a preserve where it is prohibited to take natural bits and pieces. Do not use *found* feathers in projects; you can purchase them in a craft store.

Explore, make, wear, or give these unique bark earrings. Provide art materials in an "art materials buffet" so that participants have choices about the bits and pieces that will go into the decorative aspects of the jewelry. Participants can make the jewelry for themselves, for use as gifts, or for fund-raising.

Gr. 8–12
$$ out of $$$$$

Tie It to the Technology!

Professional Resources

Jewelrymaking About.Com Free E-Class. http://jewelrymaking.about.com/od/miscjewelryprojectsnews/Free_Jewelry_Making_ECourses.htm
> About.Com, a New York Times company, offers an online jewelry-making course that comes through your email.

Jewelry Supply Closeouts. http://www.jewelrysupplycloseouts.com/
> This website offers inexpensive earring posts and other accessories for creating jewelry.

JoAnn Fabric and Craft Stores. http://www.joann.com
> You probably know about Michaels Arts and Crafts, but you might not know that there is another resource online for supplies and craft ideas for teens. Click "projects" for project ideas.

Resources for Young Adults

Balmain, J., & Traig, J. (2001). *Crafty girl: Cool stuff*. San Francisco: Chronicle Books.
> Fun, teen-appealing crafts for teen girls. This is one in a series of craft books by Jennifer Traig.

E-How Make Jewelry Videos. http://www.ehow.com/videos-on_4045_make-jewelry.html
> This website features 15 videos by craftsperson Debra Windsong on how to make, design, and even sell jewelry.

Figure 7–5: Peel the bark

Figure 7–6: Create the shape

Figure 7–7: Attach the bark

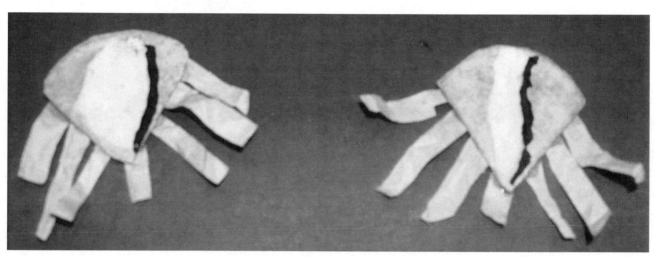

Figure 7–8: Bark earrings

NOTES

_____

_____

_____

_____

_____

LET'S GET PHYSICAL: WEIGHTS

These simple and unique weights give teens a creative outlet and something that they can use practically.

Program Suggestions

Let's Get Physical @ the Library. Make It Physical: Weight Lifting for Tweens and Teens.

What You Will Need

2 round plastic bottles (Soda companies sometimes release very round bottles for promotions during football season, to market reality shows such as *American Idol,* and you will find similar bottles used as juice containers. You can use any plastic soda or water bottle.)

Black paint and brush

White paint for highlights

Duct tape (standard size)

Sand (1 to 2½ pounds per bottle)

Glue gun

Box cutter

Wooden dowels or bamboo sticks

Step-by-Step Instructions

1. Remove labels, clean, and dry two empty plastic bottles prior to the workshop.
2. Paint the outside of the bottles. Mix a little white into a separate container and brush onto the outside of the bottle to create highlight effects. Let dry.
3. Fill the bottles with sand and close lids tightly. Cut two small slits in each bottle near the opening. Insert a wooden dowel or bamboo stick the length of the bottle to strengthen the grip. Fill the bottles with sand and close lid tightly. Generously glue and wrap duct tape around glued caps and sticks to hold in place.

Teaching Tips

Invite an exercise expert from a local gym or recreation center to give a presentation and show teens how to use weights.

Goop Be Gone is an effective chemical to use to remove gummy advertising.

The weight can be used as a prop in plays and in displays (without the sand).

Gr. 8–10
$$ out of $$$$$

Tie It to the Technology!

Professional Resources

Active 2 Software, EA Sport website. http://www.easportsactive.com/
　　Thinking about purchasing Active 2 software or other games? This official website by the producer of the game gives you resources and the information you need.

Everywhere Exercise App. http://www.evex.me/
　　Exercising without music can be a bore. Consider buying headsets for your group and downloading an app for each one. Your young adults will appreciate listening to the Everywhere Exercise Apple app available at this website.

Exercise for Teens—Safe Way to Exercise for Teens from About.Com.http://exercise.about.com/cs/exercisehealth/a/teenagers.htm
　　Tips, exercise overview, and advice for teens that you can use to inform and guide them.

Resources for Young Adults

Cooper, I. (1992). *The new, improved Gretchen Hubbard*. New York: Morrow.
　　Body image, losing weight, and relationships: all the topics that teen girls are interested in are contained in this fictional account of Gretchen, age 15, who goes on a journey of self-discovery.

Marie Claire Magazine. Workout playlist. http://www.marieclaire.com/health-fitness/workout-playlist/workout-songs-playlist-0609
    Some of your teens' favorite workout tunes.

Opportunity Grows. People powered gyms. http://www.opportunitygrows.com/tag/people-powered-gyms/
    This article outlines how people can create their own energy to power exercise equipment.

Schwarzenegger, A., & Hall, D. (1993). *Arnold: The education of a bodybuilder*. New York: Simon & Schuster.
    He knew at 15 years old that he wanted to be a bodybuilder and has won more titles than anyone else. See how he did it in this autobiography.

Figure 7–9: Paint the bottles

Figure 7–10: Place sticks

Figure 7–11: Cover in duct tape

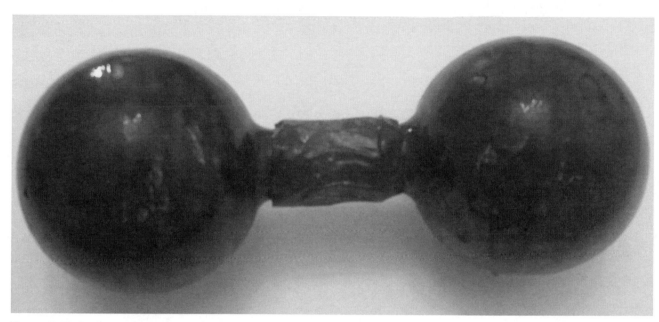

Figure 7–12: Let's get physical: weights

NOTES

_____

_____

_____

_____

_____

YOUR STATE BIRD

Each state in the United States has its own state bird. The cardinal happens to be the state bird for several different states. Each state has its own flower and flag. In this project participants create a state bird from recycled materials.

Program Suggestions

Celebrating Your State. Birds! Flowers! Flags! Bird Watching. Bird Journaling.

What You Will Need

Plastic soda or water bottle
Poster-quality paper
Paints (red, black, and white) and brushes
Tacky glue
Bark for added effects
Sandpaper

Step-by-Step Instructions

1. Use sandpaper to prepare a rough textural surface for the paint, and then paint the bottle red.
2. Cut a beak from poster board and glue it to the end of the bottle.
3. Paint details and add fallen bark to the lower body of bird.

Gr. 6–10
$ out of $$$$$

Tie It to the Technology!

Professional Resources

50 States. http://www.50states.com
> Find your state bird and flower.

National Geographic Online. Cardinal Pictures, Cardinal Facts. http://animals.nationalgeographic.com/animals/birds/cardinal/
> This website has interesting facts about cardinals and sounds.

Wikipedia. Northern cardinal. http://en.wikipedia.org/wiki/Northern_Cardinal
> The red cardinal is the state bird of seven states. Read more about them on this website. This particular *Wikipedia* entry is well referenced and is packed with diverse information about all things related to cardinals.

Resources for Young Adults

Bailey, J. (1988). *Birds of prey*. New York: Facts on File.
> Teens will enjoy this book that introduces them to birds from vultures to eagles.

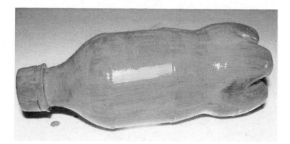

Figure 7–13: Paint the bottle

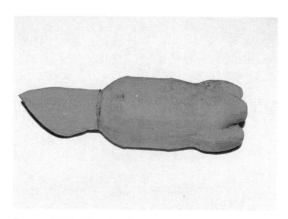

Figure 7–14: Place beak

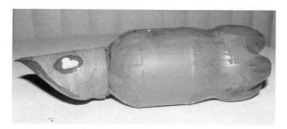

Figure 7–15: Paint details

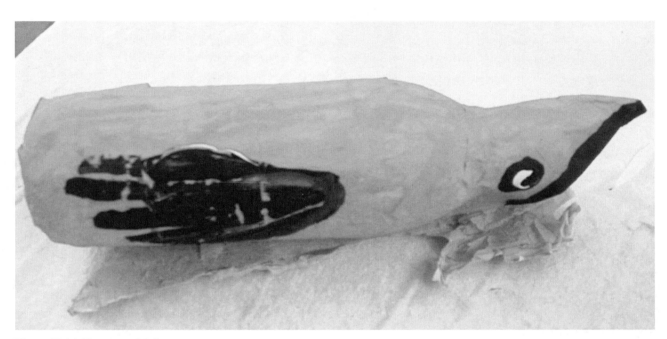

Figure 7–16: Your state bird

NOTES

_____

_____

_____

_____

_____

8

GREEN TEEN GET-TOGETHERS: ALL-NIGHTERS, AFTERSCHOOL, AND MORE

The following are ideas for art programs for those special teen times that require a bit more fun and excitement.

PROJECT LIST

T-Shirt All-Nighter	Eco Group Shadow Sculpture
Fashion Redux	Eight-Pack Soda Ring Quilt Throw
Night at the Museum	

T-SHIRT ALL-NIGHTER

Teens will use various materials and techniques to create T-shirts during this all-night party. Choose a theme or make it up as you go. Make T-shirts for fun, for a cause, or for profit.

Program Suggestions

All-Nighters. Fund-Raising at the Library. Craft Month.

What You Will Need

T-shirts (It's a good idea to buy large or X-large. Teens like oversized T-shirts.)

Variety of acrylic paints and extenders or fabric paints

Cardboard to place under the T-shirt as you paint (You can use recycled cardboard such as sturdy packaging or a recycled box.)

Foam stencils, beads, and other embellishments

Aleene's Jewel Glue, scissors, and colored chalk

Step-by-Step Instructions

1. Make it a party atmosphere.
2. Use long tables as T-shirt stations.
3. Place cardboard under T-shirt before beginning to paint or embellish it.
4. Encourage teens to lightly chalk the designs of their T-shirts.
5. Use jewel glue to attach embellishments.

Teaching Tips

Teens should apply paint lightly and apply more if appropriate. Let paints and embellishments dry completely before removing T-shirt from cardboard.

Tie It to the Technology!

Professional Sources

Nicolay, M. (2006). *Generation T: 108 ways to transform a t-shirt*. New York: Workman.
    This book is a good resource for sharing the many ways you can make a T-shirt creative to this age group.

Nicolay, M. (2009). *Next generation T*. New York: Workman.
    This book has more good ideas and a section on embellishments that will be especially helpful in working with teens on T-shirt projects.

Young Adult Resources

Instructables. Fastest Recycled T-Shirt Tote Bag. http://www.instructables.com/id/FASTEST-RECYCLED-T-SHIRT-TOTE-BAG/
    Fun and fashionable how-to on making T-shirt tote bags, all on video.

Wigand, M. (1992). *How to write and sell greeting cards, bumper stickers, T-shirts and other fun stuff*. Pleasantville, NY: Writers Digest Books.
    Teens will enjoy discovering how they can earn money selling their creative ideas.

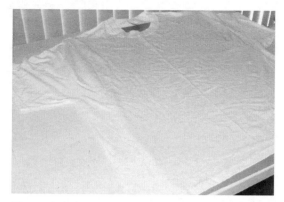

Figure 8–1: Prepare T-shirt

Figure 8–2: Paint

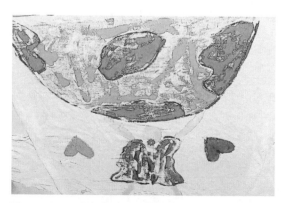

Figure 8–3: Embellish

Figure 8–4: All-nighters T-shirt party

NOTES

_____

_____

_____

_____

_____

FASHION REDUX

At "Trade Your Fashion" night, teens bring their favorite old clothing, place it in a pile, and reconstruct, repurpose, and reuse it.

Program Suggestions

Recycling. Earth Day. Trade Up Fashion Show. Dance Night@the Library (teens wear the things they made in the program).

What You Will Need

Pieces of clothing, jewelry, wallets, shoes, socks, hats, or other fashion item (Teens can be told to bring one item as the price of admission. Items should be old but clean.)
Beads, buttons, gems, fabric paints, brushes, scissors, jewelry glue, and a tape measure
Work table

Step-by-Step Instructions

1. Create a table for items. (Teens will bring their favorite old clothing and exchange it for something else).
2. Once the clothing is selected, they will revive it with patches, paints, and other embellishments.

Teaching Tips

The idea is for teens to bring items that they don't want that maybe someone else can restore and use. Do bring a few extras for those who forget or don't like the choices. Encourage boys to also participate.

Tie It to the Technology!

Professional Resources

Caroligne, M. (2007). *Reconstructing clothes for dummies*. Indianapolis: For Dummies.
    This dummy book gives suggestions for plunging in, using your imagination and not being afraid of scissors, thread, and needles. It has some T-shirt and jean ideas.

Kahn, J. (2008). *Simply sublime bags: 30 no-sew, low-sew projects*. New York: Potter Craft.
    This creative book uses shower curtains, T-shirts, pot holders, and other objects that you wouldn't think would work and turns them into bags and other objects.

Resources for Young Adults

Green Craft Magazine. http://www.stampington.com/greencraft/
    This is an arts and crafts magazine that features unique and fun projects that teens will find appealing.

Stevens-Heebner, M. (2009). *Altered shoes: A step-by-step guide to making your footwear fabulous*. Iola, WI: Krause.
    Teens will want to give their castaway shoes a second chance after they read this book that shows them how to embellish and restore their "plain janes."

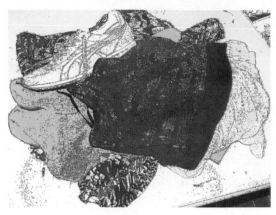

Figure 8–5: Pile of clothes

Figure 8–6: Restore

Figure 8–7: Repurpose

Figure 8–8: Fashion redux

NOTES

_____

_____

_____

_____

_____

NIGHT AT THE MUSEUM

This project involves a visit to library's custom-made museum and an all-night stay. It's all about the art at this "Night at the Museum." Turn your library into part museum and part CSI. Read a mystery novel about an art heist and then go about hiding and finding lost art.

Program Suggestions

All-Nighters. Museum Night @ the Library. Art History @ the Library. Van Gogh's Birthday.

What You Will Need

One art print for each participant (The art print should be the same title. For example, I was able to purchase several posters of *The Sunflowers* by Vincent van Gogh for about $1.00 apiece.)

Colored index cards (available at most stationary stores) to write clue questions

Step-by-Step Instructions

1. Tell the students something about the artwork and how to look at art in general.
2. Download "Questions to Ask Yourself as You Look at a Work of Art" at my website, http://www.artmuseums.com/questions.htm.
3. Introduce the art of your artist through an art print. Tell teens about the painting and show them the book display you have created about the artist.
4. Hide the art posters in the library and create a treasure hunt map that leads teens to the art posters in 10 steps.

Teaching Tips

You can purchase art prints in quantity on e-Bay (www.ebay.com). Search for your artist in Art Posters-wholesale and you will find good bargains.

You can also find art prints at your local museum store, Michaels Arts and Crafts, and Walmart.

Invite an art expert to the class to talk about the painting you have selected. Docents from your local art museum are often happy to visit and tell teens about the collection.

Along with teaching teens how to look at art, add hands-on studio art projects that reinforce the ideas that are presented.

Gr. 8–10
$$ out of $$$$$

Tie It to the Technology!

Professional Resources

Art Terms. http://www.artmuseums.com/artterms.htm
> I've included commonly used words on this website that will be helpful in talking and writing about art.

How to Look at and Write about Art. http://www.artmuseums.com/questions.htm
> Teens will learn an easy-to-understand method for looking at and talking about art.

Resources for Young Adults

Boser, U. (2010). *The Gardner Heist: The true story of the world's largest unsolved art theft*. New York: Harper Paperbacks.
> Teens will learn about the value of art on both a monetary and an aesthetic level and the criminal activity that is unfortunately part of the high-stakes art world.

Müller, M., Tatzkow, M., & Wiesel, E.(2010). *Lost lives, lost art: Jewish collectors, Nazi art theft, and the quest for justice*. Foreword by R. Lauder. New York: Vendome Press.
> Some of the most well-known collectors lost their fortunes and art and sometimes their lives simply because they were Jewish. This book follows the fight to retrieve art that was lost and taken during World War II by the Nazi regime.

ECO GROUP SHADOW SCULPTURE

Bring your group together with this bigger-than-life light assemblage. Using throwaway and found objects, teens create a sculptural environment that is a work in process.

Program Suggestions

Avant-Garde!!! Sculpture@the Museum. Art History@the Museum.

What You Will Need

Pencils and sketch paper

Found objects (Ask each person to bring an object from home that would be considered a throwaway. The size or shape doesn't matter.)

A screen or a blank wall

A table and an overhead project or other bright light source

Step-by-Step Instructions

1. You will need groupthink for this project.
2. Place all recycled items on the table.
3. Arrange objects so that you can get a general idea of what the artwork would look like as a shadow. For instance, your original idea may be a tree, castle, buildings, and so on.
4. Project the light behind the images so that the objects cast a strong shadow.
5. Experiment. The key is to create an artwork even if it doesn't look like your original concept. Encourage teens to move the objects around to create innovative shadows.

Teaching Tips

Use crumpled recycled boxes, cups, and papers to add accents and interest to the object-oriented sculpture.

Take a video or picture of the final product. Be sure the room is dark to create a strong contrast.

Gr. 8–12

$ out of $$$$$

Tie It to the Technology!

Professional Resources

Environmental Graphetti. Incredible Shadow Art Created from Junk. http://www.environmentalgraffiti.com/featured/incredible-shadow-art-created-from-junk/12265

It's a pile of junk, no wait, it's a silhouette of a couple. There are many more examples of this fascinating shadow art from this article at Environmental Graffiti.

Think or Thwim. Tim Noble and Sue Webster. http://thinkorthwim.com/2007/09/21/tim-noble-and-sue-webster/

See examples of spectacular and sophisticated art made with junk and a light source.

Treehugger. Amazing Art Created from Trash. http://www.treehugger.com/galleries/2009/02/amazing-art-created-from-trash.php?page=1

Jellyfish made out of plastic bottles, a giant roadside roadrunner made of tennis shoes and other junk are just two of my favorites from this art junkie website that features many artists. Your teens will want to create their own self-portrait after seeing the one in this collection.

Resources for Young Adults

Almoznino, A. (2002). *The art of hand shadows*. Mineola, NY: Dover.

This easy-to-understand Dover book presents simple instructions for creating hand puppets.

Make Shadow Puppets! Weekend Projects Video. http://www.youtube.com/watch?v=iPRjIIQsSAk

This easy-to-follow video takes you through the process of creating shadow puppets. Although a more traditional art form, it has some of the same elements as creating shadow art with junk.

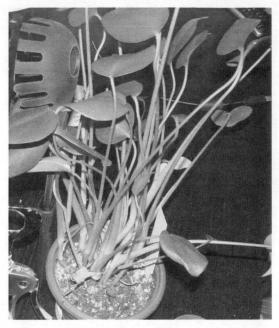

Figure 8–9: Gather objects

Figure 8–10: Arrange

Figure 8–11: Light projection

Figure 8–12: Eco group shadow sculpture

NOTES

_____

_____

_____

_____

_____

EIGHT-PACK SODA RING QUILT THROW

Many wildlife are injured by the plastic rings used to sell, organize, and carry bottles of soft drinks and water. This project uses those plastic throwaways before they get caught on the necks and bodies of unsuspecting wildlife. In this project teens will make a quilt throw that can be used on a table, piece of furniture, the wall, or the floor.

Program Suggestions

All-Nighters. Protecting the Environment. Earth Day.

What You Will Need

Fabric remnants
Discarded glossy papers
16 eight-pack plastic rings used to carry soda and water bottles (per person)
Scissors
Chalk
Aleene's Tacky Glue
Glue gun and glue

Step-by-Step Instructions

1. Using a pencil, with the plastic rings as a guide, measure and trace circles onto the fabric and discarded glossy papers.
2. Cut the fabric and papers.
3. Glue (using tacky glue) various fabric circles onto the set of 16 plastic rings that have been collected for each participant.
4. Next, glue the glossy paper circles onto the fabric with tacky glue.
5. Use the glue gun to reinforce the fabric edges. Let dry.
6. Glue all sets of plastic rings together with the glue gun to form a quiltlike throw. Let dry.
7. Embellish with buttons, jewels, or other found objects.

Teaching Tips

Use the quiltlike throw as a wall hanging or lay it on furniture or the table. Remind teens to cut plastic rings before disposing of them to protect wildlife.

Tie It to the Technology!

Professional Resources

Department of Transportation—Pennsylvania. Litter factsheet. http://www.dot.state.pa.us/Internet/pdkids.nsf/Fact Sheet?OpenForm
> This fact sheet, designed for children but informative for everyone, outlines why litter is a problem and why such trash as plastic six-pack rings is dangerous to animals.

Environmental Protection Agency. *Water Drops.* http://www.epa.gov/waterscience/learn/files/drops2.pdf
> This newsletter worth reading from the Environmental Protection Agency suggests cutting the plastic rings or yokes that are attached to soda/water and other plastic bottles and drink cans.

Young Adult Resources

Associated Content from Yahoo. Plastic 6 Pack Plastic Rings—Environmental Threat. http://www.associatedcontent.com/article/5751032/plastic_sixpack_rings_environmental_pg2.html?cat=57
> This article presents a well-written outline of why plastic rings are dangerous to the environment and gives specific examples of what happens when this type of pollutant is irresponsibly discarded into the environment.

Martha Stewart. Snowflake video. http://www.marthastewart.com/article/6-pack-snowflake
> Watch this video and follow the instructions to make a unique snowflake artwork out of plastic rings.

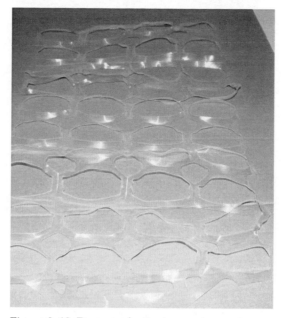

Figure 8–13: Prepare plastic rings

Figure 8–14: Cut fabric and papers

Figure 8–15: Embellish

Figure 8–16: Eight-pack soda ring quilt throw

NOTES

_____

_____

_____

_____

_____

9

GOING LOCAL AND GLOBAL: INTERNATIONAL, COMMUNITY, AND INTERGENERATIONAL ART PROJECTS

These art programs enable teens to understand and experience their role as citizens of their country, community, and world. Projects take one hour to create unless otherwise specified.

PROJECT LIST

Cats and Dogs: Art for a Cause	Christmas around the World
Picasso-Inspired International Green Cards	Zulu Love Bead Doll

CATS AND DOGS: ART FOR A CAUSE

Being green means taking care of the environment and its creatures. The mistreatment of cats and dogs is an issue we can do something about. Sponsoring a fund-raiser for your local pet shelter is one way teens can help.

Program Suggestions

Animal Awareness Day@the Library. Dog Days of Summer. Art@the Library.

What You Will Need

#2 drawing pencils

Soft erasers

Paper stump (available in art stores, used for smearing and creating value gradations)

Q-tips for blending

Drawing paper, 8½ by 11 inches: one to two sheets per teen

Newsprint (a cheaper drawing paper) for practice

Step-by-Step Instructions

1. Ask teens to bring photos of their pets or visit a local animal shelter and ask to take pictures of animals.
2. Invite a local teacher or graduate student to the library to demonstrate basic drawing skills.
3. Encourage teens to use the resources later onto learn basic drawing skills.
4. Have teens draw their chosen animal.
5. Place drawings on black construction paper and hang in library.

Teaching Tips

Invite local artists to draw the pets of library visitors at the library for a donation to the library. Library patrons can donate money to the local shelter.

Tie It to the Technology!

Professional Resources

Brookes, M. (1991). *Drawing for older children and teens: A creative method that works for adult beginners, too*. New York: J. P. Tarcher.
   This is a book about drawing and a resource for those who teach drawing. Learn drawing techniques that you can pass on to your group.

Edwards, B. (1989). *Drawing on the right side of the brain: A course in enhancing creativity and artistic confidence*. New York: J. P. Tarcher.
   Edward's book is a highly popular and classic how-to-draw book with a creative twist.

Resources for Young Adults

About.Com Drawing Step-by-Step Draw a Cat. http://drawsketch.about.com/library/bl-step-cat.htm

About.Com Drawsketch—Pet Photography—How to Photograph Your Pet. http://drawsketch.about.com/od/learn todrawanimals/ss/petphotography.htm

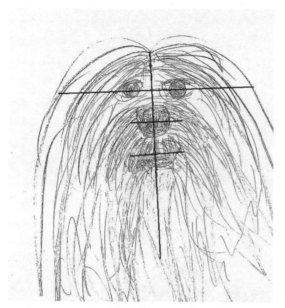

Figure 9–1: Establish lines using photo

Figure 9–2: Erase lines

Figure 9–3: Add professional shading

Figure 9–4: Hang and exhibit

NOTES

_____

_____

_____

_____

_____

PICASSO-INSPIRED INTERNATIONAL GREEN CARDS

Community service is important for teens and for others. In this program seniors and others who could benefit from interaction and activities come together in a fun and meaningful green art project inspired by the artwork of Picasso.

Program Suggestions

Community Service. Art History. Celebrating Creativity. Picasso's Birthday. Meet the Generations.

What You Will Need

Contact a local senior center or facility that invites activities groups to participate with their community. Organize a volunteer activity visit with the center.

Locate and purchase a poster of one of Picasso's best-loved artworks, *Mains-Aux-Fleurs* (*Hands with Flowers/Bouquet*). See resources.

Black construction paper, 8½ by 11 inches (2 sheets)

Fabric remnants (to use as center of flowers): You will need three 1 inch by 1 inch fabric round pieces and one ½-inch circle that will serve as the center of the flower. Cut stems from recycled paper. Stems and petals should be cut from fabric in various sizes from 1 to 3 inches in length. You may want to precut these pieces so that your program fits a one-hour framework.

Aleene's glue and scissors

Various colored papers (yellow, red, blue) or multicolored paper from magazines and other recycled paper sources such as junk mail, copy paper toss-aways, and so on

4 pieces white copy paper

Pencils and soft erasers

Step-by-Step Instructions

1. Be sure to explain the activity in detail to the program director of the facility. Ask for advice concerning special challenges and accommodations for the participants. Communicate those needs to your teens.

2. Ask for special tools that may be available to seniors such as specialty scissors and so on.

3. Plan the same kind of atmosphere at the center as you would at the library. Bring food and fun to the event, but be sure to ask the program director for advice about what kind of foods, music, or other program materials to bring.

4. Organize supplies prior to the event. Be sure to make one example before the event so that you clearly understand the project and any problems you may encounter. Make provisions for a missing participant: Be ready to stand in or make other accommodations. This project requires two people, preferably a teen and senior. At the center, pair one teen with one senior.

    a. Encourage teens to introduce themselves and encourage seniors to talk about themselves and their interests.

    b. Set up the table beforehand so that all products are available to participants. Materials should be distributed so that all supplies are available to each group of two rather than using a buffet-style arrangement.

    c. First, teens should trace or ask the senior to trace the senior's hand twice onto the white paper. Next, the teen should trace or ask the senior to trace the teen's hand twice. Encourage seniors and teens not to be too concerned with perfection. Sometimes the rugged edges in art are the most appealing. Traced hand drawings should then be cut out. Be sure to be aware of anyone who may need help and ask program director of the center for help in identifying those who may need assistance.

    d. Be sure that you have made available a copy of *Mains-Aux-Fleurs* to the group. Place the hands onto the composition first. The senior's hand tracing should be at the bottom of the composition, with the palm placed down. Place the teen hand tracing about a little more than midway toward the top. Fold the teen tracing at the wrist to give a three-dimensional effect with the palm facing upward.

    e. Place stems, petals, and centers of flowers onto the paper prior to gluing. Creativity should abound so there is not one particular way to place the flowers.

5. Each participant will have an artwork to keep and hang.

Tie It to the Technology!

Professional Resources

Artcyclopedia—Picasso. http://www.artcyclopedia.com/artists/picasso_pablo.html
> You will find everything you and your teens want to know about Picasso at this website. It includes museums where you will find Picasso's artwork.

Fulcrum Gallery. http://www.fulcrumgallery.com/Pablo-Picasso/Mains-Aux-Fleurs_26652.htm
> This is one of the places you can see and purchase a copy of the painting for $25.00. Look for specials from this quality online gallery. You can also find posters at your local Michaels Arts and Crafts, JoAnn Fabrics, Aaron Brothers, Walmart, museum stores, and other favorite places to buy art supplies.

Resources for Young Adults

Alternative Solutions—Intergenerational Programming. http://www.activitytherapy.com/intergen.htm
> This website is a good resource outlining a number of programs and organizations that illustrate how seniors and teens are getting together in a variety of creative and rewarding ways.

In the Mix—PBS. Bridging the Years . . . Teens and Seniors Mix It Up! http://www.pbs.org/inthemix/educators/lessons/bridgingtheyears_guide.pdf
> Helpful article describes a program that helped teens develop relationships with seniors, resulting in a breaking down of stereotypes and other benefits for both.

Northside Eastside Senior Coalition. http://www.nescoinc.org/intergenerational.html
> This website shows how teens are making a difference in the lives of seniors. There are many good ideas and inspirations for your own community.

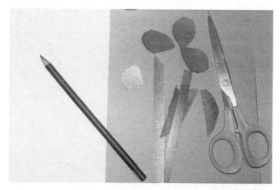

Figure 9–5: Gather materials

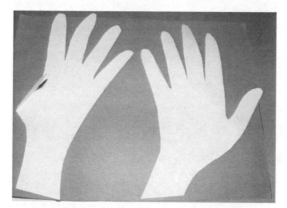

Figure 9–6: Place hands

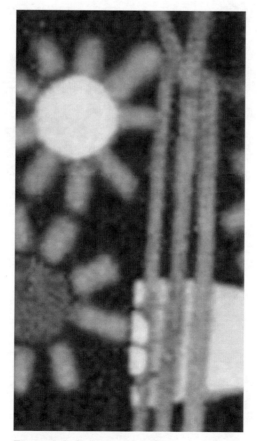

Figure 9–7: Stems and petals

Figure 9–8: *Mains-Aux-Fleurs*

NOTES

_____

_____

_____

_____

_____

CHRISTMAS AROUND THE WORLD

Christmas is celebrated by many people all around the world. Make eco-friendly Christmas decorations reflecting the many countries that celebrate Christmas. Teens can decorate a tree using the decorations. Create a display that contains a write-up with a short fact sheet about each country and how it celebrates this holiday.

Program Suggestions

Christmas around the World. Bon Voyage! Meeting Teens around the World.

What You Will Need

Natural objects to make Christmas decorations such as cinnamon sticks, pine cones, eucalyptus and other natural branches, fallen leaves, acorns and other nuts, dried flowers, cranberries and other berries, cooked popcorn, peppermint sticks, and so on

Found objects such as used CDs, clothespins, buttons, bottle caps, bows, fabric scraps; paper from magazines, junk mail, discarded books, and other sources of discarded paper; and small packages such as mini cereal boxes, mint tins, and so on

Glitter created by placing magazine paper, silver gum wrappers, shining packing materials, and so on into a blender for several seconds until you get the effect you want (designate the blender for crafts)

Papier-mâché balls (to use instead of Styrofoam balls; see instructions)

Tacky glue, scissors, and a variety of acrylic paints and brushes

Step-by-Step Instructions

1. This would work well as a two-part program. In the first workshop ask teens to research a country or place that interests them.
2. Ask them to do some exploring and find out whether and how that unique area celebrates Christmas.
3. Teens can choose to create a replica of an ornament they find interesting or use the location as inspiration for a unique ornament they develop on their own.
4. Ask them to make a wish list of supplies that they might need to create their decoration.
5. In the second workshop ask teens to sketch their ornament, and then create it with the materials that you have supplied.

Teaching Tips

Create a group memory book that includes facts about the countries, teen sketches, and photos of the event and the final completed Christmas tree.

Gr. 8–12

$$ out of $$$$$

CHRISTMAS DECORATION BALLS

What You Will Need

2 by 2 inch newspaper squares (torn, not cut) and additional newspaper to place project on to dry

Cup of flour

Water (½ cup)

School glue (2 tablespoons)

Balloons (small)

Paper towel for blotting and wiping mixture from hands

From *Teens Go Green!: Tips, Techniques, Tools, and Themes for YA Programming* by Valerie Colston. Santa Barbara, CA: Libraries Unlimited. Copyright © 2012.

Step-by-Step Instructions

1. Mix flour and water to the consistency of pancake batter. You don't want the mix to be lumpy or too thick, but you don't want a runny mixture either.

2. Add glue to help bind the mixture.

3. Blow balloon and tie end.

4. Dip newspaper squares into mixture and cover balloons with them. Use a paper towel to blot excess mixture. Be sure the entire balloon is covered.

5. Let dry completely. This may take an entire day. Once dry, it's ready to paint and decorate.

Tie It to the Technology!

Professional Resources

Christmas around the World. http://www.42explore2.com/xmas.htm
    This is a good overall Christmas resource that includes educational as well as arts and crafts websites.

White House Christmas Tree Tradition. http://www.christmastree.org/whitehouse.cfm
    This White House resource has many interesting facts about the White House Christmas tree including how long it takes to grow a Christmas tree and information about the recycling status of the Christmas tree provider.

Resources for Young Adults

Canfield, J., Victor, M., & Newmark, A. (2008). *Chicken soup for the soul: Christian teen talk: Christian teens share their stories of support, inspiration and growing up.* Cos Cob, CT: Chicken Soup for the Soul.
    Good selection of short nonfiction articles dealing with God, family, teen struggles, friends, values, and other things important to teens.

Christmas around the World. http://teens.librarypoint.org/Christmas_around_the_world
    Resources for writing a paper, arts and crafts, and other Christmas references at the Rappahannock Regional Library in Virginia.

Figure 9–9: Papier-mâché ball

Figure 9–10: Decorate

Figure 9–11: Hang

Figure 9–12: Christmas around the world decoration

NOTES

_____

_____

_____

_____

_____

ZULU LOVE BEAD DOLL

Teens create an African-inspired sculpture (with a Zulu love letter bead theme) using toss-away beverage bottles. The people of Africa have been creating objects from recycled materials for a very long time as teen will learn in the resources provided.

Program Suggestions

Be There Teens—Africa. Trash to Treasure. Art and Literacy.

What You Will Need

Plastic soda, water, or juice bottle (orange juice bottles work well for this project)

Acrylic black and white paint

Paint brushes

Various colors of construction paper

Scissors and glue

Twine

For the head, a Styrofoam ball or ball made of papier-mâché (see Christmas decoration activity for ingredients)

Step-by-Step Instructions

1. Paint plastic bottle with black Paint. Let dry.
2. Cut and glue small pieces of twine to represent the wire coils that are representative of the Zulu women's beaded neck jewelry.
3. Glue various colors of construction paper onto the twine in small pieces to represent colored love beads. Teens should place colored paper "beads" to convey a love letter. (See resources.)
4. Use twine and paints to accessorize the figure in unique styles. Each participant should decorate it depending on his or her own interests and styles.
5. Share and discuss the "love letter" with the group.

Gr. 8–10
$ out of $$$$$

Tie It to the Technology!

Professional Resources

Indigoarts Website. Recycled Arts and Toy Bazaar. http://www.indigoarts.com/store1_recycle_3.html
   See toys, baskets, dolls, mini motorcycles and cars made from tin, telephone wire, and bottle caps from Africa, Viet Nam, and South America

Zulu Beadwork Homepage. http://minotaur.marques.co.za/clients/zulu/index.htm
   You will find good examples of Zulu styles at this website. There is also the Zulu color code that presents the various meanings of the colors that are used in this beaded love letter.

Resources for Young Adults

Christian Science Monitor. In Africa, a papercraft path out of poverty. Poor Ugandan women turn their lives around by handcrafting for BeadForLife, a small Colorado-based nonprofit group. http://www.csmonitor.com/2007/1031/p13s01-woaf.html/(page)/2
   This article outlines how the Bead for Life (http://beadforlifestore.org/) organization helps fight poverty in Africa. Women make a variety of jewelry from recycled magazines and sell them through the organization online.

Fitzgerald, D. (2007). *Zulu inspired beadwork: Weaving techniques and projects*. Loveland, CO: Interweave Press.
   This book is a colorfully illustrated comprehensive look at Zulu beadwork.

Figure 9–13: Paint container

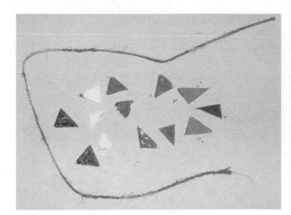

Figure 9–14: Paint beads and twine

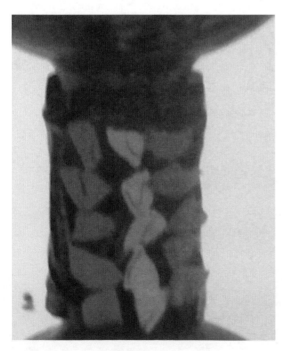

Figure 9–15: Accessorize and share bead letter stories

Figure 9–16: Zulu love bead doll

NOTES

_____

_____

_____

_____

_____

10

EARTH DAY AND OTHER CELEBRATION IDEAS ALL YEAR LONG

This chapter provides easy-to-access art and programs ideas for celebrating Earth Day and other ecological themes.

PROJECT LIST

Go Global Eco Globes

Architecture in a Box: Design a New Architectural Style and Future City Using Packaging Material

Globe-Trotting Habitat Float

Under-the-Sea Creatures

Water Fountain—Table Style

Save a Squirrel

GO GLOBAL ECO GLOBES

Create your own eco globe using a balloon and papier-mâché. Accentuate the land and water masses to show how all is connected.

Program Suggestions

Earth Day. Recycling. Environmental Awareness. Art@the Library.

What You Will Need
Newspaper (2 full-size sheets per teen)
Balloon
Variety of blue, brown, and green acrylic paints

Papier-mâché mixture (Mix 1 cup flour + 1 cup water + 2 tablespoons glue, slowly pouring water into flour.)

Step-by-Step Instructions

1. Tear newspaper print into 2-inch strips and dip into papier-mâché. Cover the inflated balloon. Let dry. It may take an entire day.

2. Paint the globe using colors to identify the topographical landscape.

Gr. 6–8
$ out of $$$$$

Tie It to the Technology!

Professional Resources

Greenspan Worldwide. http://www.greenspanworld.org/environmental_club_network.htm
   This is the resource you need for creating an environment club. Network with others who have already formed one from around the world.

Volunteers for Peace. http://www.vfp.org/teenCamp.html
   This organization pairs teens and adults who want to volunteer to improve their world with hands on projects. Teens are placed (with parent's permission and a fee) in local and international communities. A peace blog, volunteer project list, and more information about this program is available at their website.

Resources for Young Adults

National Geographic World Music. http://worldmusic.nationalgeographic.com/
   Teens will learn about the culture of teens and others around the world through their music and videos on this website.

Test Your Geographical Knowledge (The Oceans and Continents). http://www.lizardpoint.com/fun/geoquiz/worldquiz.html
   How much do you know about geography? Test your knowledge about the world and individual continents. Lots of fun! Teens can make it a group game.

Figure 10–1: Papier-mâché

Figure 10–2: Paint object

Figure 10–3: Add details

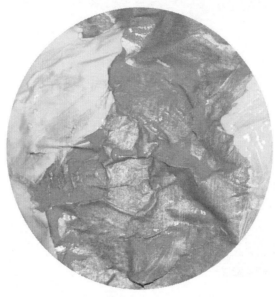

Figure 10–4: Go global eco globes

NOTES

_____

_____

_____

_____

_____

110

ARCHITECTURE IN A BOX: DESIGN A NEW ARCHITECTURAL STYLE AND FUTURE CITY USING PACKAGING MATERIAL

Program Suggestions

Architecture as Art. Trash to Treasure. Imagine It@the Library.

What You Will Need

Foam and cartons from packaging of various boxes

Variety of papers from recycled sources—magazines and junk mail

Assortment of acrylic paints and brushes

Buttons, bottle caps, fabric remnants, twine, nuts, and bolts

Aleene's Tacky Glue or Mosaic Glue

Step-by-Step Instructions

1. Ask teens to bring those funny-shaped packaging shapes (foam and sturdy paper) that we normally throw away. If you take a second look at them, you will see that they have distinct shapes that often appear architectonic.
2. Encourage teens to create unique architectural features from their imagination.
3. Place structures together to form a recycled city.
4. Use paper squares to create a mosaic effect.
5. Paint "murals" on the packaging to replicate urban buildings.

Gr. 8–10

$$ out of $$$$$

Tie It to the Technology!

Professional Resources

About.Com Architecture. Top 8 Free Lesson Plans & Activities. http://architecture.about.com/od/teachersaids/tp/lessonplans.htm

> Bring architecture into the classroom with these fun, free lesson plans. The site offers unique architecture projects that can be modified for teens.

Braun-Reinitz, J., Goodman, A., & Weissman, J. (2009). *On the wall: Four decades of community murals in New York City*. Jackson: University Press of Mississippi.

> This informative book takes you on a tour of the community murals of New York City that tell you much about the city and culture.

Resources for Young Adults

How to Look at Architecture. http://www.artmuseums.com/architecture.html

> Author's website that gives tips for looking at architecture.

Lindsey, D., Karlitz, G., & Rauf, D. (2005). *Career ideas for teens in architecture and construction*. New York: Ferguson.

> Practical and informative book for those interested in the possibility of careers in the architectural and construction world.

Lee, J. Ames. (1991). *Draw 50 buildings and other structures: The step-by-step way to draw castles and cathedrals, skyscrapers and bridges, and so much more*. New York: Broadway.

> Easy-to-follow instructions for creating a variety of architecture structures.

Figure 10–5: Various shapes

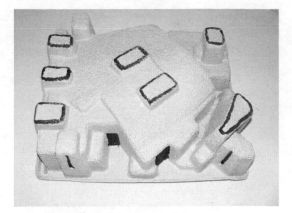

Figure 10–6: Paint

Figure 10–7: Embellish

Figure 10–8: Architecture in a box

NOTES

_____

_____

_____

_____

_____

GLOBE-TROTTING HABITAT FLOAT

Create a habitat box for one of the various animal habitats (grasslands, ocean, desert, wetlands, etc.) across the world. Learn about the habitats of various countries of the world. Use a shoebox and found objects to create various habitats. Create a display and exhibit the habitats in the library.

Program Suggestions

Earth Day International. Make It a Parade! World Travelers.

What You Will Need

Shoeboxes (just ask your favorite manager at your shoe, big box, or department store)

Materials such as moss, sticks, rocks, and recycled magazines (nature type work well) and paper, including paper bags

Colored markers, colored pencils, various paints, and brushes

Step-by-Step Instructions

1. Ask teens to select a habitat—grasslands, ocean, desert, or wetlands—and research what animals live there.
2. Duplicate the environment imitating items and landscape.

Teaching Tips

Discuss the definition of *habitat* and ask teens to define the local environment in which they live. Set up the display as a parade, for example, Pasadena Tournament of Roses Parade.

Figure 10–9: Materials

Figure 10–10: Environment

Figure 10–11: Embellish

Figure 10–12: Globe-trotting habitat float

NOTES

_____

_____

_____

_____

_____

UNDER-THE-SEA CREATURES

Use recycled bottles, fast-food plastic, and soft foam to create sharks or other amazing underwater creatures.

Program Suggestions

Sharks. Saving the Oceans. Earth Day.

What You Will Need

A small fine-grade piece of sandpaper for each project
Plastic bottle
Silver, black, and white acrylic paint and brushes
Foam from takeout fast food and soft foam craft sheets available from most arts and crafts supply stores
Tacky glue and scissors

Step-by-Step Instructions

1. Use sandpaper to rub the plastic bottle prior to painting it to give it a rough texture.
2. Paint the plastic bottle of your choice.
3. Create the shark's or other creature's head using foam and recyclables and glue.
4. Place head over the top of the bottle and glue. The bottle will float.

Teaching Tips and Special Instructions

Encourage teens to use their imaginations and create other fantastical creatures.
Optional: Purchase a plastic battery-operated engine from a hobby store and attach to shark.

Gr. 6–10
$$$ out of $$$$$

Tie It to the Technology!

Professional Resources

4D Vision Great White Shark Anatomy Model by Tedco
    At $25.00 this model is worth its price as it allows teens see the Great White up close and personal. Good for general knowledge and as a model for drawing.

National Gallery of Art. "Watson and the Shark: The Story." http://www.nga.gov/feature/watson/story1.shtm
    Teach them about art. Learn about the famous painting *Watson and the Shark* by John Singleton Copley at the National Gallery of Art.

Resources for Young Adults

Ames, L. (1991). *Draw fifty sharks, whales, and other sea creatures.* New York: Three Rivers Press.
    Good resource for drawing sharks, whales, and other sea creatures.

Compagno, L., Dando, M., & Fowler, S. (2005). *Sharks of the world.* Princeton, NJ: Princeton University Press.
    Teens will appreciate the scope of information in this field guide to sharks with the theme of shark conservation.

Nature's Perfect Predator—Great White Shark. YouTube. http://www.youtube.com/watch?v=yp9YKEO9e1w
    Teens will enjoy this informative Discovery TV video that shows the strength and aggression of the Great White shark while teaching about its anatomy.

Figure 10–13: Paint the body

Figure 10–14: Create the head

Figure 10–15: Attach head

Figure 10–16: Undersea creature

NOTES

_____

_____

_____

_____

_____

WATER FOUNTAIN—TABLE STYLE

Use a salad bowl to create a group tabletop water fountain.

Program Suggestions

Water Awareness. Relaxation and Meditation. Earth Day.

What You Will Need

Water fountain pump kit, available at home improvement stores and online

Clear tubing. Use the smaller width size. You will need to purchase about 1 foot. It is fairly inexpensive. You will find this tubing at Home Depot, Loews, or other home improvement stores.

A medium-size salad bowl. A sturdy clear type would be interesting, but a solid color would also work.

For embellishment, recyclable plastic plants and flowers blended with real plants such as ivy that don't need soil to grow, as well as shells, rocks, and other natural and found objects

Step-by-Step Instructions

1. Install the fountain according to the manufacturer's instructions and warnings.
2. Decorate the inside of the bowl using natural designs and motifs. Fill with plants and rocks and other embellishments.

Teaching Tips

Make it a group project.

Involve everyone in suggesting ideas for designing the fountain.

Make more than one.

Take a look at resources to see a variety of water fountains for inspiration.

Gr. 8–11
$$$ out of $$$$$

Tie It to the Technology!

Professional Resources

Old Fashioned Living. Tabletop Water Fountain. http://oldfashionedliving.com/fountains.html
> This website gives you some interesting and simple instructions and ideas for creating a tabletop fountain.

Sunterra. http://www.sunterrausa.com/home
> This website is a supplier of small and large fountain components. You can't buy products from this website, but you can see how they work and what is available. Sunterra and other manufacturers' fountain pumps can be ordered online through Amazon.com for as little as $10.00.

Resources for Young Adults

Cusik, Dawn. (2000). *Table top fountains: 40 great easy and great looking projects to make*. Ashville, NC: Lark Books.

How to Make a Water Fountain with Host John Mangana. http://www.videojug.com/film/how-to-make-a-water-fountain
> This video will answer questions teens may have about making a simple water fountain.

Figure 10–17: Gather materials

Figure 10–18: Attach pump

Figure 10–19: Create layout

Figure 10–20: Group water fountain

NOTES

_____

_____

_____

_____

_____

SAVE A SQUIRREL

When artists design a package or container, they don't always understand their impact on the environment and animals. For example, yogurt containers are notorious for getting stuck on the little heads of squirrels. In this project teens will learn something about ecologically sound product design while creating cool packaging.

Program Suggestions

Endangered Animals. Product Design. Art@the Library.

What You Will Need

Pencils and soft erasers
Drawing paper, 8½ by 11 inches
Colored markers
Empty yogurt containers (various brands)

Step-by-Step Instructions

1. Make a display of the yogurt containers.
2. Discuss product design. What are the possible design problems that could have an impact on wildlife? How do the narrow openings of some yogurt containers present a problem to squirrels?
3. Ask teens to create a design that would be more eco-friendly.
4. Use pencils and colored markers to make the final product.
5. Brainstorm ways in which the yogurt containers can be recycled. Make a project using one of the ideas presented in another workshop.

Teaching Tips

Have a design contest at the library that focuses on eco-friendly designs.

Gr. 6–12
$ out of $$$$$

Tie It to the Technology!

Professional Resources

Incredible Art Department. http://www.princetonol.com/groups/iad/lessons/high/Cindi-dream.htm
    Lesson plan asks teens to create an American Dream product.

Squirrel with yogurt container on head. YouTube. http://www.youtube.com/watch?v=yyVNREfyM2s
    This is one of many videos that show a squirrel with a yogurt container with a narrow opening stuck on its head.

Resources for Young Adults

Environ-Mom. 101 Uses for Yogurt Cups. http://www.enviromom.com/2007/05/101_reuse_ideas.html
    Good ideas for recycling yogurt containers.

Treehugger. Packaging Design at It's Worst. http://www.treehugger.com/galleries/2009/07/packaging-design-at-its-worst.php?page=10
    Slideshow illustrates examples of using plastic, paper, and other materials for preserving, presenting, and shipping.

Sketch out some ideas.
Create a number of
designs.
Remember that the
opening of the
container needs to be
wide.

Figure 10–21: Design sketch #1

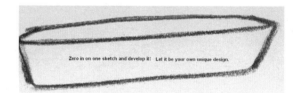

Zero in on one sketch and develop it! Let it be your own unique design.

Figure 10–22: Design sketch #2

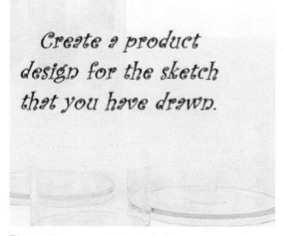

Create a product design for the sketch that you have drawn.

Figure 10- 23: Design sketch #3

Save the Squirrels

Figure 10–24: Design for yogurt container

NOTES

_____

_____

_____

_____

_____

11

BOOKS INTO ART PROGRAMS

These art programs and art projects take about one hour to complete, and correspond to popular environmental teen fiction and nonfiction.

PROJECT LIST

Neighborhood Bird Study Program—Audubon Style

The Teen Guide to Global Action

Photographing the Wetlands (or Other Natural Wonders)

The Green Machine and the Frog Crusade

Trash to Treasure Arts Party

Generation Green

Green Jobs: What and Where Are They?

It's Your World—If You Don't Like It, Change It

NEIGHBORHOOD BIRD STUDY PROGRAM—AUDUBON STYLE

Lewis, Barbara. (2008). *The Teen Guide to Global Action: How to Connect with Others (Near & Far) to Create Social Change.* Free Spirit Publishing. 135 pages.

Written for the "we" generation who understand the importance of local and international service and the power of communities and youth to achieve big-enough goals to make a global impact, this nonfiction book provides the youth services librarian and teen reader an opportunity to explore the world of service and an outline for practically tackling problems such as human rights, hunger and homelessness, health and safety, education, promotion of tolerance, and the environment and conservation.

Make It a Program

Neighborhood Bird Study Program—Audubon Style. James Audubon's (1785–1851) goal was to paint and document every bird in America. This project demonstrates to teens how to use simple pencil techniques to create a basic bird shape and introduces Audubon, the well-known bird artist and ecologist, to the group by organizing a study of local bird life.

Use Audubon drawings and actual field study site sketches to inventory and document local birds. Teach simple drawing techniques and conservation while celebrating the birthday (April 26) of the naturalist and artist James Audubon at your library. Introduce your group to endangered bird species through posters, the Audubon website, or an *Audubon Field Guide* book.

What You Will Need
Drawing journals (ask teens to bring their own)

Pencil and soft eraser

Fine-point black pen

Step-by-Step Instructions
1. Distribute "How to Draw a Bird" handout. (See Figure 11–3.)
2. Draw along with your group.
3. Suggest observing and documenting local birds.
4. Share a book that illustrates Audubon's artwork.

Gr. 6–12

$ out of $$$$$

Teaching Tips

Encourage teens to observe birds in the wild and to use pen-and-ink artwork to create illustrated journals and paintings of birds indigenous to their own neighborhoods.

Listen to birds and learn to recognize bird sounds using Internet resources.

Organize an art exhibition in the library, using bird sounds as background music.

Teens should be encouraged to give tours and create marketing materials such as invitations, flyers, and catalogs for the art exhibition.

Invite an artist to demonstrate basic drawing techniques or follow the easy instructions in Figures 11–2, 11–3, and 11–4 and let teens experiment with their own styles.

Tie It to the Technology!

Professional Resources

Bull, J. L. (1994). *National Audubon Society field guide to North American birds—E: eastern region* (rev. ed.). St. Louis: Turtleback.
This field guide is a good resource for reading and sharing with teens, especially those living in the eastern region.

Farrand, J., Jr., & Udvardy Miklos, D. F. (1994). *National Audubon Society field guide to North American birds, western region.* St. Louis: Turtleback.
A field guide to read and share with those living in the western region.

National Audubon Society. http://www.audubon.org/nas/
This website is an outstanding resource for you and your teens. You will find teaching tips and many other resources about bird conservation.

Official State Birds. http://www.50states.com/bird/
Gain an appreciation for your state bird and create a program using your own state bird.

Resources for Young Adults

Adventures in Bird Watching. Host Ken Dial. Janson Media. 2004. DVD.
  Originally a television series, this documentary presents the travels of Ken Dial through the United States and Costa Rica exploring bird cultures up close.

E-Nature: Bird Audio. http://www.enature.com/birding/audio.asp
  Hear and practice hundreds of common American bird sounds.

Girl's Life. How Teens are Helping in the Gulf. http://www.girlslife.com/post/2010/06/21/teens-aid-animals-in-the-gulf.aspx
  Article points to young teens who are making a difference when it comes to helping the birds of the Gulf Coast.

Figure 11–1: Drawing journal

Figure 11–2: Sketches

Figure 11–3: Sketch and notes

Figure 11–4: Journal entry

NOTES

_____

_____

_____

_____

_____

TRASH TO TREASURE ARTS PARTY

Sivertsen, Linda, & Sivertsen, Tosh. (2008). *Generation Green*. Simon Pulse Publishers. 272 pages.
> This book is filled with awesome ideas for this age group. One idea is an art party. This project is a slight modification of it.

Program Suggestions

Art@the Library. Book to Art. Earth Day.

What You Will Need

> This isn't just any kind of party. Teens will visit a lake, river, ocean, park, or other nature setting and volunteer for a one-hour cleanup. Throw the obvious trash away, but bring back any items that can be cleaned such as bottles, toys, plastic containers, or other usable surprises. Provide gloves, trash picker sticks, a bag for trash, and one for treasures. Contact your local city administration for rules, regulations, and permits and to set up the cleanup.

> After the cleanup . . .

> Collect all found objects and plan a cleanup arts and crafts party. First, ask teens to clean the objects (be sure to use gloves) with detergent and set the objects on a table. Brainstorm as a group. What can be made from these objects? Provide paint, glue, brushes, and other items that teens may need to redo these treasures into sculptures, assemblages, jewelry, or other reusables. Let imaginations soar.

Teaching Tips

> Create a display that features the *objects d'arte*. Include photos of the day of the event and what the objects looked like prior to their makeover.

Tie It to the Technology!

Professional Resources

Leisure Arts. (1998). *Aleene's something from nothing: Treasures from trash*. Little Rock, AR: Leisure Arts.
> Aleene is one of the original trash-to-treasure experts. This book features flea market finds and gifts for yourself and others from Aleene and her daughters.

Leisure Arts. (2004). *Trash to treasure*. Little Rock, AR: Leisure Arts.
> There are many ideas that are inexpensive and suitable for teens in this creative book.

Resources for Young Adults

Chute, James. Artist defies stereotypes, can't be categorized: Pattern and decoration is just one element in Kim MacConnel's range of playful art. *San Diego Union Tribune*, Sign on San Diego website. http://www.signonsandiego.com/news/2010/oct/16/beyond-the-pattern/
> This article outlines the work and philosophy of San Diego artist Kim MacConnel, who has collected and used plastic beach throwaways for more than three decades.

> Artist note: Kim MacConnel was my art professor many years ago at the University of California, San Diego. We made a lot of fun projects in the class including turning the classroom into a pool environment using art as our only tool.

Taylor, T. (2009). *Eco books: Inventive projects from the recycling bin*. New York: Lark Books.
> This is an interesting book for teens. The author uses what many would consider garbage to create artwork.

Figure 11–5: Found object

Figure 11–6: Recycled

Figure 11–7: Renewed

Figure 11–8: Recycled trash-to-treasure object

NOTES

_____

_____

_____

_____

_____

134

PHOTOGRAPHING THE WETLANDS (OR OTHER NATURAL WONDERS)

Stephen Tchudi. (1987). *The Green Machine and the Frog Crusade*. Delacorte Books for Young Readers. 221 pages.
> How brave is David? Does he stick to his fight to save the wetlands even though it means going against the status quo and his own relative?

Program Suggestions

This project uses the medium of photography. Teens use their digital cameras to photograph rare plants, animals, and the general environmental health of the marshlands, ocean, mountains, or other natural wonders of their area.
> Art Exhibition@the Library. Art@the Library. Earth Day.

What You Will Need

Digital cameras

Computers for teens to upload and print their photographs

Library meeting room

Exhibition space

Step-by-Step Instructions

1. Teens (grades 10–12) meet in the library to discuss exploring their surroundings for areas of eco-interest. In teams of four to six, teens explore, photograph, and exhibit topics of their choice, such as local watersheds, rare plant species, clean or polluted waterways (oceans, rivers, streams), local wildlife, green schools, or other interesting environmental themes.

2. Meet at the library to print out photographs and arrange an exhibition.

3. Teens should organize the meeting times, locations, and exhibitions, but there should be a Youth Services Librarian overseeing and acting as an advisor for the group.

4. Optionally: Provide a digital camera (on loan) for any groups that may not have one of their own. Ask Friends of the Library or another organization for funds to purchase inexpensive digital cameras for teens.

Gr. 10–12
$$$$ out of $$$$$

Tie It to the Technology!

Professional Resources

Environmental Protection Agency. *Service Learning: Education beyond the Classroom*. http://www.epa.gov/osw/education/pdfs/svclearn.pdf
> This is an excellent resource for adults wanting to share service learning ideas with their groups. There are specific examples of actual student projects.

Resources for Young Adults

Creech, Steve. (2006). *Hold your water: 68 things you need to know to keep your planet blue*. Riverside, NJ: Andrew McMeel.
> Find practical ways for conserving water.

Environmental Protection Agency. Adopt a Watershed. http://www.epa.gov/owow_keep/adopt/index.html
> Teens learn how they can protect their local watersheds and how other teens are doing it in their own areas.

Figure 11–9: La Jolla coast California

Figure 11–10: Seagull over ocean

Figure 11–11: Seagull in flight

136

Figure 11–12: Sea lions on beach

NOTES

_____

_____

_____

_____

_____

GREEN JOBS: WHAT AND WHERE ARE THEY?

Halpin, Mikki. (2004). *It's your world—if you don't like it, change it*. New York: Simon Pulse Publishers. 304 pages.

> If teens have a passion, this book is for them. The author gives many concrete ideas for getting socially involved. This project uses a different medium and helps teens to develop communication skills.

Program Suggestions

In this program teens will conduct an interview, videotape it, and publish it. There is a lot of talk today about green jobs—but what are they? What is a green job, and how do you train for it? What green jobs are available in your city?

> Video@the Library. Making a Difference. Book to Art.

What You Will Need

Teens will need an advisor for this project.

> Announce the program and set up a meeting with teens to introduce it.
>
> Teens should do some research in the library before they decide who to interview. Encourage teens to contact their local employment agencies, colleges and universities, and businesses.
>
> They will need equipment such as a video recorder and the use of Windows Movie Maker. Instructions for using this easy-to-understand software are available on YouTube (www.youtube.com).
>
> Teens can use the YouTube website to publish their videos. Easy-to-follow instructions are available on the website. The library should sign up for the service.
>
> Teens can create a Facebook (www.facebook.com) account or blog (www.blogger.com) to publish the information they acquired in the research and interviews. The library should register for these services.

Step-by-Step Instructions

Video is an important medium for teens interested in their world. Encourage teens to have an action plan. They should:

1. Have an overall plan for the project—a beginning and an end.
2. Look at each interview as a separate project. Limit the interviews to four experts.
3. Arrange specific meeting dates at the library. The Youth Services Librarian should oversee the teens' progress.
4. Make it clear to the person being interviewed that their comments will be quoted on the blog and that they will be asked to be videotaped and published on YouTube. Advise teens to create a release form that states that they have permission to videotape and publish the video.
5. Keep taped interviews somewhat brief (less than five minutes) and focused on the questions regarding the definition, training, hiring, and availability of green jobs in your area.

Tie It to Technology!

Professional Resources

Green Collar Blog. http://www.greencollarblog.org/

> This website is an excellent resource for jobs, training, and news updates for those interested in green jobs.

Problogger. http://www.problogger.net/archives/2008/03/17/create-a-video-tutorial-and-help-others/

> This is a helpful blog that discusses video blogging and includes references for easy-to-use, helpful software such as Camtasia.

Resources for Young Adults

Deitsche, S. (2010). *Green collar jobs: Environmental careers for the 21st century*. Santa Barbara, CA: Praeger.

> This book is very comprehensive, outlining green jobs in areas you might not have first considered, including international jobs.

Green jobs for a new economy. (2010). Lawrenceville, NJ: Petersons.

Index

After Juice Aftershave (fast-food container project), 50
Antonelli, Monika, 3
Architecture in a Box: Design a New Architectural Style and Future City Using Packaging Material project, 111
Art club, 19
Art history resources and supplies, 6
Asbestos risks, 8

Books into art programs: Green Jobs: What and Where Are They?, 138; Neighborhood Bird Study Program—Audubon Style, 128; Photographing the Wetlands, 135; project list, 127; Trash to Treasure Arts Party, 132
Books with green theme ideas, 14
Brushes, books, art instruments (supplies), 6
Brushes, storage of, 4

Camouflage Catch All (eco-friendly art activity), 44
Cats and Dogs: Art for a Cause project, 92
Christmas around the World project, 99–100
Club creation, 19–20
Crafts materials and supplies, 6

Dancers Paper Style (eco-friendly art activity), 34
Desktop Organizer with Fake Spill (under $1 art project), 64

Displays for marketing: carbon footprint display, 20; plastic bottle fountain, 20–22
Documentation of activities, 13
Drink It and Grow It: Plant It in the Library (fast-food container project), 53

Earth Day and other celebrations: Architecture in a Box: Design a New Architectural Style and Future City Using Packaging Material, 111; Globe-Trotting Habitat Float, 114; Go Global Eco Globes, 108; project list, 107; Save a Squirrel, 123; Under the Sea Creatures, 117; Water Fountain—Table Style, 120
Eat It! Paint It! (fast-food container project), 56
Eco-friendly one hour art programs: Camouflage Catch All, 44; Dancers Paper Style, 34; Fabulous Paper Fashion, 28; Music Box (from a recycled book), 40; project list, 27; Recycled Cars, 37; Sassy Grassy Grass Portraits, 31
Ecology club, 19–20
Eight-Pack Soda Ring Quilt Throw activity, 88
Entertainment value of programs, 13
Exhibitions for marketing, 23

Fabulous Paper Fashion (eco-friendly art activity and program), 28

Fashion Redux project, 81
Fast-food container projects: After Juice
    Aftershave, 50; Drink It and Grow It:
    Plant It in the Library, 53; Eat It! Paint
    It!, 56; Gumball or Candy Machine
    Replica, 59

Get-together projects: all-nighters, after-
    school, more: Eco-Group Shadow
    Sculpture, 85; Eight-Pack Soda Ring
    Quilt Throw, 88; Fashion Redux, 81;
    Night at the Museum, 84; project list,
    77; T-Shirt All-Nighter, 78
Global and local art projects: Cats and
    Dogs: Art for a Cause, 92; Christmas
    around the World, 99–100; Picasso-
    Inspired International Green Cards,
    95–96; project list, 91; Zulu Love
    Bead Doll, 103
Globe-Trotting Habitat Float project, 114
Glues and attachments (supplies), 5
Go Global Eco Globes project, 108
Greening the library, ten steps, 3–4
Green Jobs: What and Where Are They?
    program, 138
The Green Library Movement: An Overview
    and Beyond (Antonelli), 3
Green themes: books/website with theme
    ideas, 14; "green" words search, 13;
    searching stacks online, 13–14; Voice
    of Youth Advocates website, 14
Gumball or Candy Machine Replica (fast-
    food container project), 59

"Health & Safety Website" (City of Tucson),
    12
Heavy metals risks, 8

Library club, tips for creating, 20
Likes and dislikes of teens, 11–12

Marketing programs: club creation, 19–20;
    displays, 20–22; exhibitions, 23;
    resources for marketing, 23–24;
    virtual displays, 23
Media necessities and supplies, 5
Miller, Kathryn, 3
Music Box (eco-friendly art activity), 40

Neighborhood Bird Study Program—
    Audubon Style program, 128
Night at the Museum project, 84

OEHHA Guidelines for the Safe Use of Arts
    and Crafts Materials (2007), 8
Organic solvent risks, 8

Paper items, storage of, 4
Paper necessities and supplies, 4–5
Parents (adults): activities for promotion,
    23; as recycled materials resource, 7
Photographing the Wetlands (or Other
    Natural Wonders) program, 135
Picasso-Inspired International Green Cards
    project, 95–96
Princeton Library website, 3
Professional resources: books into art pro-
    grams, 128, 132, 135, 138; Earth Day
    and other celebrations, 108, 111, 114,
    117, 120, 123; eco-friendly one hour
    programs, 28, 31, 34, 37–38, 41,
    44–45; fast-food container projects,
    50, 53, 56, 59; green teen get-
    togethers, 78, 81, 84, 85, 88; one hour
    eco-friendly programs, 28, 31, 34,
    37–38, 41, 44; under $1 art projects,
    64, 67, 70, 74
Program suggestions: After Juice After-
    shave project, 50; Architecture in a
    Box, 111; Camouflage Catch All activ-
    ity, 44; Cats and Dogs: Art for a Cause
    project, 92; Christmas around the
    World project, 99–100; Dancers
    Paper Style activity, 34; Desktop
    Organizer with Fake Spill activity,
    64; Drink It and Grow It: Plant It in
    the Library activity, 53; Eco-Group
    Shadow Sculpture activity, 85; Eight-
    Pack Soda Ring Quilt Throw activity,
    88; Fabulous Paper Fashion activ-
    ity, 28; Fashion Redux project, 81;
    fast-food container projects, 50, 53,
    56, 59; Globe-Trotting Habitat Float
    project, 114; Go Global Eco Globes
    project, 108; Green Jobs: What and
    Where Are They? program, 138; Let's
    Get Physical: Weights, 70; Music Box
    activity, 41; Neighborhood Bird Study
    Program—Audubon Style program,
    128; Night at the Museum project,
    84; Photographing the Wetlands,
    135; Picasso-Inspired International
    Green Cards project, 95; Recycled
    Cars activity, 37; Sassy Grassy Grass
    Portraits activity, 31; Save a Squirrel
    project, 123; Under the Sea Creatures
    project, 117; Trash to Treasure Arts
    Party program, 132; T-Shirt All-
    Nighter project, 78; Water
    Fountain—Table Style project, 120;
    Way Cool Bark Jewelry, 67; Your State
    Bird project, 74; Zulu Love Bead Doll
    project, 103

Promotion ideas, 23–24
Public Libraries Going Green (Miller), 3

Recycled Cars (eco-friendly art activity), 37
Recycled materials, 7–8
Resources and supplies, 3–8; art history, 6; brushes, books, art instruments, 6; crafts materials, 6; eco-friendly one hour programs, 28, 31, 34, 37–38, 41, 44–45; fast-food container projects, 50, 53, 56, 59; general storage, 4; glues and attachments, 5; for marketing, 23–24; media necessities, 5; paper necessities, 4–5; recycled materials, 7–8; safety necessities and supplies, 6–7; under $1 art projects, 64, 67, 70, 74. *See also* Professional resources; Young adults, resources

Safety: necessities and supplies, 6–7; resources for artists, 12
San Diego Library Visual Arts Program, 23
Sassy Grassy Grass Portraits (eco-friendly art activity), 31
Save a Squirrel project, 123
Stacks online, searching for green themes, 13–14
Storage necessities and supplies, 4

Teaching tips, for activities and projects: After Juice Aftershave project, 50; Architecture in a Box project, 111; Camouflage Catch All activity project, 44; Cats and Dogs: Art for a Cause project, 92; Christmas around the World project, 99–100; Dancers Paper Style activity, 34; Desktop Organizer with Fake Spill project, 64; Drink It and Grow It: Plant It in the Library project, 53; Eco-Group Shadow Sculpture activity, 85; Eight-Pack Soda Ring Quilt Throw activity, 88; Fabulous Paper Fashion activity, 28; Fashion Redux project, 81; Globe-Trotting Habitat Float project, 114; Go Global Eco Globes project, 108; Green Jobs: What and Where Are They? program, 138; Let's Get Physical: Weights project, 70; likes and dislikes, 11–12; Music Box activity, 41; Neighborhood Bird Study Program—Audubon Style program, 128; Night at the Museum project, 84; Photographing the Wetlands program, 135; Picasso-Inspired International Green Cards project, 96; pre-program preparation, 12; program preparation, 12–13; Recycled Cars activity, 37; revamping old techniques, 12–13; Sassy Grassy Grass Portraits activity, 31; Save a Squirrel project, 123; Under the Sea Creatures project, 117; Trash to Treasure Arts Party program, 132; T-Shirt All-Nighter project, 78; Water Fountain—Table Style project, 120; Way Cool Bark Jewelry project, 67; Your State Bird project, 74; Zulu Love Bead Doll project, 103

Teaching tips, for teaching teens: likes and dislikes, 11–12; pre-program preparation, 12; program preparation, 12–13; revamping old techniques, 12–13; theme development, 14

Technology, use of: After Juice Aftershave project, 50; Architecture in a Box project, 111; Camouflage Catch All activity project, 44; Cats and Dogs: Art for a Cause project, 92; Christmas around the World project, 99–100; Dancers Paper Style activity, 34; Desktop Organizer with Fake Spill project, 64; Drink It and Grow It: Plant It in the Library project, 53; Eco-Group Shadow Sculpture activity, 85; Eight-Pack Soda Ring Quilt Throw activity, 88; Fabulous Paper Fashion activity, 28; Fashion Redux project, 81; Globe-Trotting Habitat Float project, 114; Go Global Eco Globes project, 108; Green Jobs: What and Where Are They? program, 138; Let's Get Physical: Weights project, 70; Music Box activity, 41; Neighborhood Bird Study Program—Audubon Style program, 128; Night at the Museum project, 84; Photographing the Wetlands program, 135; Picasso-Inspired International Green Cards project, 96; Recycled Cars activity, 37; Sassy Grassy Grass Portraits activity, 31; Save a Squirrel project, 123; Under the Sea Creatures project, 117; Trash to Treasure Arts Party program, 132; T-Shirt All-Nighter project, 78; Water Fountain—Table Style project, 120; Way Cool Bark Jewelry project, 67; Your State Bird project, 74; Zulu Love Bead Doll project, 103

Teenagers. *See* Young adults; Young adults, resources

Trash to Treasure Arts Party program, 132
T-Shirt All-Nighter project, 78

Under $1.00 art projects: Desktop Organizer
    with Fake Spill, 64; Let's Get Physi-
    cal: Weights, 70; project list, 63; Way
    Cool Bark Jewelry, 67; Your State
    Bird, 74
Under the Sea Creatures project, 117

Voice of Youth Advocates website, 14

Water Fountain—Table Style project, 120
Websites: artwork, displays, exhibitions, 20,
    23; artwork and exhibitions, 23;
    blogging ideas, 16; craft supplies, 6;
    eco-friendly one hour programs, 28,
    31, 34, 37–38, 41, 44–45; fast-food
    container projects, 50, 53, 56, 59;
    green theme ideas, 13, 14; health-
    oriented booklists, 3; library club
    creation, 20; media resources, 15;
    professional resources, 8; recycled
    materials, 7; resources for artist
    safety, 12; toxic materials, 8; under

$1 art projects, 64, 67, 70, 74; video
    broadcasting, radio station creation,
    17; workspace design, 16
Workspace design: assistance of teens, 15;
    blogs with ideas, 16; green space
    resources, 16; radio station creation,
    16; themes, 15

Young adults: help with space design, 15;
    ideas for volunteering, 19–20; likes
    and dislikes, 11–12; tips for teaching,
    11–14
Young adults, resources: books into art pro-
    grams, 127, 132, 135, 138; Earth Day
    and other celebrations, 108, 111, 114,
    117, 120, 123; eco-friendly one hour
    programs, 28, 31, 34, 37–38, 41, 44–45;
    fast-food container projects, 50, 53,
    56, 59; green teen get-togethers, 78,
    81, 84, 85, 88; one hour eco-friendly
    programs, 28, 31, 34, 38, 41, 45; under
    $1 art projects, 64, 67, 70, 74
Your State Bird (under $1 art project), 74

Zulu Love Bead Doll project, 103

ABOUT THE AUTHOR

VALERIE COLSTON lives in Southern California and is a professor at American Public University System. She also teaches as an adjunct professor at the Art Institute of Pittsburgh's Online Division. She graduated with a BA from the University of California, San Diego, and an MA in Art History from San Diego State University. Ms. Colston is the author of *200 Projects to Strengthen Your Art Skills*, published by Barrons Educational Services, 2008. She is the creator of the award-winning "Art Teacher on the Net," at www.ArtMuseums. com and YouthLibrarians.com—both art resource websites for teachers and youth librarians. Ms. Colston has been conducting children and teen library workshops at libraries for several years. Her highly recommended *Art for Youth Librarians* workshops have been attended by librarians from across the United States and internationally.

Edwards Brothers, Inc.
Thorofare, NJ USA
December 7, 2011